SECRET WEAPON

Men Overcoming Chaos

by
**Lt. Col. Dave Winecoff
USMC (Ret.)**
with Chuck Dean

WinePress Publishing **WP** *Mukilteo, WA 98275*

AUTHOR'S NOTE

In 1982 I read a statistic that shocked me. It said that three times as many Vietnam veterans died of suicide in the eight years after the war's end as had died in combat during that ten-year war. For the first time I realized how deadly the civilian life (the aftermath of combat) can be for some. Originally my desire was to write a book to help veterans struggling with the effects of PTSD (post-traumatic stress disorder). I have now come to realize all of life is in a sense a combat zone. My one-word definition for combat is "chaos." We all are exposed to intervals of "chaotic" times while living our life.

All who volunteer or are drafted into the armed forces come from the civilian world. One telling key as to how well men will do in the military is the home from which they come.

As a modern-day centurion, I offer this book to share valuable life lessons learned both in combat situations and in civilian life. Centurion means "captain of one hundred." In my third combat tour I was a Marine captain leading an infantry company of about 170 Marines.

Jesus Christ marveled to his civilian disciples at the faith of a centurion soldier in chapter eight of the book of Matthew. Faith is absolutely essential to success in combat. On the eve of his death Jesus wondered aloud if He would find faith on the earth when he returns. Even in the New Testament times the very first convert outside the Jewish community was Cornelius, a soldier.

Thirteen years beyond my military career I find that my picture of the Commander and Chief is quite different from that of most in the church who have never had the military experience. Most do not think of Jesus Christ as a military man. My view of Him is fashioned more from how He appears in chapter nineteen of the book of Revelation and by who He chose to be leaders in the Old Testament works (Moses, Joshua, David).

The civilian church in America is complaining about the growing moral decay which is so evident. Yet no civilians seem to see the connection of this breakdown to ending the military draft in our nation. This "no draft" policy violates Scripture. Why? Because military experience helps the family to instill discipline into the next generation's children.

Another equally bad social experiment adopted by civilian leadership is the no-fault divorce policy. This was a major blow not only to the American family, but also to the fighting capability of America's military by discouraging soldiers whose families had broken up. Yet, the church is still not protesting either decision.

For the spouse who does not wish a divorce, "no fault divorce" is a direct violation of that party's right to "due process" as guaranteed in the U.S. Constitution. Desertion is to an army as divorce is to the family—a form of rebellion. If a parent can unilaterally break a contract with another parent in marriage when the going gets tough, how will that impact upon an adult child of divorce when the going gets tough for him in combat?

How do civilian decisions such as "no fault" divorce and ending the draft affect our long-range ability to survive as a nation? Adversely!

I frequently hear civilians say that the "Cold War" has ended and we are now the world's only superpower. In only eight of the 500 great battles of antiquity did the country with the numerically superior force win. Smaller nations in history have won against larger forces with telling frequency. Israel in the Old Testament shows many examples. A number of smaller nations can gang up on a larger nation. I am concerned about how naive we are as a nation. There are forces abroad that consider America to be the "Great Satan." Is there anything that civilians can learn from a centurion? I hope so!

Semper Fidelis,

David F. Winecoff
Lt. Colonel USMC (Ret.)
Nam Vet three tours

DEDICATION

This book is dedicated to the sons and daughters of Vietnam-era veteran parents.

ACKNOWLEDGMENTS

Special thanks to my immediate family, especially my now grown children, Mary, Mark, Steven, and Scott, for bearing with their dad through the ordeal of writing this book. Thanks to all who read through my progressive manuscripts and commented. I especially want to thank veterans who God placed before my eyes as examples who endured, overcame afflictions and difficulties to accomplish their visions and dreams. Among them are Bill Bohannan, executive director of Christian Armed Services Association (CASA) of Everett, Washington, Jim Brewer of Orlando, Florida, David Courson, past director of Christian Emergency Relief Team (CERT) of San Diego, California, Chuck Dean, past director of Point Man Ministries of Mountlake Terrace, Washington, and Oli North, director of Freedom Alliance, Washington D.C. Lastly, I want to say thanks to unnamed friends too numerous to mention.

Contents

Part One

Earning One's Credentials

AN ARROW IN THE QUIVER

"Like arrows in the hand of a warrior are the sons of one's youth. Happy is the man whose quiver is filled with them."
Psalm 127:4-5a

The first hands to touch me were Chinese.

As sometimes happens with a military wife, Dad was not around when Mom needed his comfort. August 12, 1939 was one of those times. I'm told I arrived in Shanghai, China on a warm summer day. Dad was in north China manning a river gunboat that was keeping tabs on the war raging between the Japanese and Chinese armies in various parts of China. His U.S. Marine Corps duty had become a priority and had taken precedence over family needs.

The two men around when I was born were a Chinese doctor and the Marine who had driven mom in a staff car through two Japanese occupation zones to get her to the Chinese hospital. The 4th Marine regiment had contingency plans at that time to evacuate our dependents into the hills when the Japanese attacked. The situation later worsened. Shortly after we left China at the end of dad's three-year tour, the Marine Corps made the policy decision to send all dependents home. Thus began my life as the child of a third generation U.S. Marine officer. In light of my subsequent military experience it seems fitting that I would first appear on the scene not far from the front lines of war.

From what I heard the delivery was a normal one. I'm sure somewhere in the journals of that Shanghai hospital there still exists some evidence of a Chinese doctor recording my birth for the record. He probably got all of fifty cents for his services.

Once after being told about Mom being rushed to the hospital in a Marine staff car with me on the way, I asked her how she was treated by the Japanese soldiers who stopped them at the four checkpoints she journeyed through. "They were very considerate and hurried us right through," she laughed. "They could clearly see the nature of the problem."

This attitude was to change drastically over the next several years when the Japanese broadened their horizons with the attack on Pearl Harbor and on the Philippine Islands where the Marine Brigade had been reassigned in the year after our departure. My parents knew Marines who died in that heroic struggle at Corrigador, and of course, Marines who died and those who survived the infamous Bataan death march. Thank God my family was spared that ordeal.

Soon thereafter, because of the deteriorating situation in China, the 4th Marine Regiment was reassigned to the Philippines. Later, they became the only Marine unit to ever be surrendered when, after a nine-month fight, half a million Americans were surrendered to the Japanese army in the Philippines. It became a strategic impossibility to sustain that force after our naval losses in the Pacific starting with Pearl Harbor.

COLORFUL FIGURES

I come not only from a line of valiant men, but adventurous women as well. Not long after I first cried out to greet life, my great-grandmother at 92 accompanied my grandmother out to China to see her first great-grandson. En route, the ship they were traveling on pulled into Japan for a stop. After being denied the right to take cameras ashore they snapped off many shots from the portholes of their stateroom. As the story goes in our family circles, these same photos were later used in target selection during the Allied bombing of Japan. I wondered as a child if their journey to see me wasn't just a cover for "sensitive" reasons that were more in the national interest than my birth. Looking over my family tree of colorful figures I would not be surprised. My great-grandmother died on the way home and was buried at sea.

COLONEL CHALLACOMBE

My mother's maiden name was Challacombe. On her side of the family was my uncle Art Challacombe, Jr., also a Marine officer. His father, Colonel Art Challacombe, Sr. was a dynamic Marine.

Art Sr. got commissioned out of a two-year West Point class on July 11, 1917 and was sent immediately to Europe to fight in the Great War (WW I). By the time that war had ended in 1918 he had an indecent number of medals on his chest for a junior officer. He later added to them with tours of overseas duty in Santa Domingo, Haiti, Nicaragua, and Cuba where Art, Jr. was born. He retired in 1946 leaving behind a legacy that testifies to the type of man he was. My speculation is the only reason that he didn't walk away from the service with the

Congressional Medal of Honor is because he didn't get killed in the line of his gallant duty as a Marine.

He did earn the Navy Cross, the nation's second-highest award for valor while serving in Nicaragua. The story only confirms the odyssey of one Art Challacombe. Here is the official awards order that accompanied his medal:

"Awarded: Navy Cross for distinguished service in the line of his profession as a member of a special mission that was organized for the purpose of executing the plan for the disarming of the troops of the Liberal party of the Republic of Nicaragua. The duty was satisfactorily accomplished between the dates of 12 May-15 May 1927, and in the face of great difficulties in the nature of troops to the no. of over two thousand being on the verge of open mutiny at the prospect of delivering their arms, open threats against his life and having to safeguard a large sum of government money in his safekeeping. By the successful accomplishment of his mission, Captain Challacombe did much to lessen the severity of the banditry then rife in the country."

Like many military commendations for honorable deeds written hurriedly during chaotic times, this one only gives a brief overview of what actually happened. The story is much more interesting. Art was stationed in Nicaragua during the period called the "Bandit Wars," and he single-handedly devised a brash plan to end the war that was in progress. He thought about it, talked about it, and continually brought it before his peers every chance he got. Finally his superiors captured the spirit behind this hair-brained idea and took him up on it.

He detailed out his entire plan for the command which in simple form went something like this: "Give me $50,000 and I'll go out there and buy all the guns that the bandits have. Without guns they can't very well fight any longer. I'll take a squad of Marines to pull security on the money, and we will travel the major river tributaries by canoe, visiting every village along the way. I'll buy up all the guns I can at twice their worth. If we can't end this war militarily, then why not through economics?"

His operating scheme was approved and launched. After their first stop at a village the word went out like wildfire across the country that some crazy gringo was offering everyone big money for their guns. The armed guerrillas, their bandit wives and girlfriends, and every other Nicaraguan hastened to the villages along their route to see if the offer was real. The bandits' thinking was sell one, buy two; while the women were thinking that the men could buy a new gun and they would spend the difference.

The genius portion of the entire scheme was yet to unfold. As soon as Challacombe launched his buying trip, a strict naval embargo was instituted to stop any illegal gun running opportunities from capitalizing on this new profit-making opportunity. The plan was to keep that embargo in effect long enough that the money would be spent on more peaceful pursuits. Bandit activity dropped off to nothing just as Art Challacombe, Sr. had predicted, thus earning him instant fame and a hero's medal. Art was a man's man, and I cherish the few times I heard indirectly such exploits while growing up on posts and stations around the Corps.

THE FOLKS

Georgians seldom had any occasion to hear about a small outfit like the Marines in 1935. Without television news, ideas and concepts were slow in coming forth. My Georgia-born father had never heard of the Corps until a retired army colonel living next door in Atlanta advised him to give it a try.

Dad was in the Army ROTC class at the University of Georgia, and had been offered a regular commission with the Marine Corps as one of the two top graduates during a difficult budget year when the army was only offering reserve commissions. When he sought counsel on what to do, the elderly colonel next door told dad that the Marines had a solid future and to accept the offer. He did, and was a dedicated career Marine until infectious hepatitis forced his retirement in 1961 after 27 years of service. By that time he had many awards and honors for his service in WW II, Korea, and in his post-war duties.

Mom came into the picture in 1937. Dad was stationed aboard the U.S.S. Texas, a battle cruiser which was dry-docked in Bremerton, Washington for nine months before shipping out to the Far East. She was voted by her classmates the prettiest girl in her Everett senior high school class, and it didn't take Dad long to discover her and win her over with his deep southern accent and charm. Soon Dad was reassigned to a three-year tour in the China regiment. After a year in college Mom followed him to China and they were married over there.

The first year of my life in Shanghai was spent with a Chinese amah (nurse) also attending to me. I had plenty of motherly love. One aspect of overseas duty back in those days was that a married second lieutenant earning $18 a month could easily afford servant help in China. The amah, according to Mom, was not only able to care for me, but her entire family on the household allowance she was given to take care of our family.

My first birthday happened twice. I was on board a ship headed for America. Of course I don't remember, but the day we crossed the international date line (12 August 1940) I turned one year old. Since the clock is set back 24 hours on that line, my first birthday was celebrated by ship's crew twice. The ship's cook baked two cakes for the occasion.

GROWING WITH THE CHANGES

SEA SHELLS: A SEA STORY

Around the time I was nine years old I became curious about war, and began to ask Dad a lot of questions. He never did get into the gory details about his combat duty on Guadalcanal, Okinawa, and other places of war renown; but on one memorable occasion he did tell a war story that satisfied my curiosity.

As a youth Dad spent a lot of pleasant summers down around Sea Island, Georgia. He loved to collect seashells, and took this hobby with him to the Solomon Islands as a Marine. On his off-duty time he spent hours strolling the beaches collecting shells that he would send home as keepsakes.

During one of these off-duty excursions, on a supposedly secured island, he wandered alone up the beach in search of shells. As his thoughts of home absorbed him, he reminisced of the carefree Georgia summer days that he longed for. Suddenly he was brought into present time by the stark reality of imminent danger. Fear spread through him like a cold shot of electricity as he stood looking eyeball-to-eyeball with four silent, ragged-look-

11

ing armed Japanese soldiers. They began moving slowly out of the tree line towards him on a skirmish line, weapons at the ready. With nothing else as a possibility, he quickly drew his pistol and dashed for the water. Clinging to a solid log which was floating just off shore, he brandished the pistol at the men. While keeping away from them in the water he could tell that they very much wanted to shoot him but were afraid that the sound might bring other Marines down on them. After much discourse and debating, they silently melted back into the jungle. When it was good and dark, he waded ashore and returned to camp a soggy, but far wiser man.

I loved that sea story. Not only did it satisfy my urge to know more about war, but it added a lot of value to our Solomon Island seashell collection.

Dad's distinct flare for handling potentially explosive situations always stands out as I read and hear about his service as a Marine. When he was in Korea he personally wrote up the battle plan for the famous withdrawal of the 1st Marine Division from the Chosen Reservoir in 1950. After the actual withdrawal he was flown out and assumed command of the 11th Marine Artillery Regiment.

His replacement was Carl Youngsdale, a future general in the Corps. Dad pulled Youngsdale from a crashed plane, saving his life, and it was a wonderful feeling to read a letter that he wrote my Dad after a major engagement while serving in Vietnam. Here is a portion of that letter which was written soon after I received the Silver Star there in combat:

Dear Buzz:

"Today I saw the bravest man I have ever known and I know he was brave because I was standing right beside him." The brave young man this time was a son of another Marine who used to return to the 11th Marine CP in Korea and repeat the above phrase to Jim Appleyard and myself. I was reminded of those days by the presentation of the Silver Star Medal to young Captain Winecoff by Bill Buse during his last visit to Vietnam. Your young Marine looks great and as the award indicates, he is doing a great job. He was decorated for taking his company through the boondocks, setting up an ambush on an enemy controlled road, triggering the trap causing many enemy casualties without losing a Marine of his own. It was a superb job."

> C.A. Youngsdale
> Major General USMC

Needless to say, I was humbled by these gracious words that came from one of Dad's old buddies. Being the son of a popular man can do that, but being the son of a popular Marine not only humbles a guy, but it also makes him take stock of where he is going with his life .

UNCLE SAM'S FAMILY

As any military dependent can verify, living with parents who have made the service their lives can have interesting effects on their children. I've seen some military kids despise the life of frequent moves, military regulations, etc., and I've seen others like myself flourish and bloom in it, considering every move and change an adventure with valuable lessons at each turn in the road.

I was not a very verbal young man, and shyness marked my life. The only problems that I encountered with moving from base to base was the fact that I was so reticent. To compensate, I developed a love for sports. I realized that it was easy to be accepted by total strangers if you could participate in athletic games. I reached out socially to my new peers and made friends through this passion for sports, and the common bond which sports bring in relationships. I was fortunate that every base that we moved to had excellent sport facilities; after all, fighting wars definitely requires that the men who participate be in the best physical shape possible. Facilities were there for that purpose, but we dependents cashed in on them too.

The athlete who most affected my interest in sports was my dad. He loved recreational sports, and inspired all of us boys (me, Michael and Steve) to play for the many benefits we received. It was all good training for the days ahead.

ANOTHER MARINE OFFICER

It was still summer-hot at Quantico on September 4, 1962 when I reported for duty. I expected it, having lived there when I was growing up. As a student lieutenant I was ready to get down to the business of becoming the best Marine Corps officer I could be.

Basic officer courses start times in the fall of 1962 were affected by the abortive invasion of Cuba, and my start was delayed two months. Four rigorous years of pounding books at the University of Washington while living near the poverty level deterred some from woman chasing. This extra-curricular activity now began in earnest for those with delayed gratification in this area. I didn't need too much will power in this area having already met my soon-to-be future wife and so began hitting the books at Quantico in earnest. While many of the other student lieutenants were on their time off, they lounged and generally took it easy, or dated women. As for me, I had no further interest in dating. The object of my interest in the opposite sex was a couple thousand miles away also studying.

My future wife got a letter or a phone call from me on a daily basis. These were my breaks from studying. I was a young Marine in love. The phone calls to her made my heart ache more to see her again.

That Christmas I traveled to Washington State for my two-week break to be with the lady I wanted to spend the rest of my life with. Hours after arriving in the Seattle area I proposed to her and we went shopping for a wedding ring.

Upon my return I attempted to throw myself into studies with more diligence than ever. My fiancee's acceptance of my proposal gave me extra motivation to perform the best I could. My class ranking had a lot to do with where the Marines would assign me. I came out number seven in my student company and first in my platoon. This qualified me for a regular commission (as opposed to reserve) upon graduation from The Basic School. I was one happy Marine.

The excitement of receiving the commission and getting orders for my first permanent duty station in Hawaii only made me want to get back to Washington State as soon as I could. En route between Virginia and Hawaii I made a quick detour to wed. What more could a guy ask for? A three-year assignment to beautiful Hawaii accompanied by the most beautiful girl in the world. I was on cloud nine. We honeymooned on our way to Oahu, Hawaii via Vancouver, B.C., San Francisco and San Diego, California before setting sail via passenger ship. To top this off, my new assignment gave me the privilege of serving and training in Hawaii with the 4th Marine Regiment, my father's old unit in China the year I was born.

VIETNAM VOLUNTEER

In November, 1964, two years after my commissioning and a year after our wedding, two training quotas came down to 1st Marine Brigade Headquarters on Oahu.

Two infantry officers would be selected to spend a couple of months observing the combat activities of the South Vietnamese Marines in their fight against a Communist insurgency. I knew that a duty assignment like that could give me the experience and know-how to save lives later on if we (the Marine Corps) were sent in force to a combat arena. This opportunity wouldn't come along very often, I thought. Realizing the invaluable advantage this would give me as an officer leading men in combat, I volunteered.

The war in Vietnam was not well known back then, an occasional news item appeared in the papers or on TV. I had not heard much about it. There weren't any official rumors that the U.S. would be involved there in ground action in the near future. I felt that our unit would not be deployed. I therefore took the chance of going on this temporary assignment for the experience.

At the time I was the executive officer of Delta Company, 1st Battalion, 4th Marine Regiment. There were other officers more senior to me who would get the first shot at going. But I threw my hat in the circle anyway.

There was one big negative if I was picked to go-- our new daughter, Mary, was going to have her first Christmas while I would be gone, and my wife's parents were coming to visit. Surprisingly, I was chosen as one of the two officers to go. I felt that it was such a rare opportunity that I couldn't very well refuse.

OBSERVATION TOUR

As the plane descended over the Southeast Asian landscape I marveled, like so many other Americans in the years to come, at the breathtaking beauty of Vietnam. The lush greens and wide serpentine-like rivers, that glistened gray in the bright sunlight, made me think of the many travel brochures I had seen of exotic tropi-

17

cal resorts around the world. One would never believe that a vicious guerrilla war was raging in those very same beautiful jungles and rivers.

I was sent to a small hamlet six kilometers from the provincial headquarters town of My Tho on Christmas Eve of 1964. My Tho was a riverside town located several hours south of Saigon, in the Mekong Delta.

"The Delta," as many American G.I.s over the next ten years would know it, was a strategic area where fierce fighting between South Vietnamese forces and Communist aggressors raged around the clock. This vast network of waterways and rice paddies was the richest rice producing area in Asia. It has been said that the Mekong can supply rice to all of China indefinitely. This richness made war in the area intense.

I was assigned to the 4th Rifle Company, 1st Battalion, Vietnamese Marine Brigade. I was the only American among 150 Vietnamese infantrymen. One of the officers spoke a little broken English. Other than him it was sign language and gestures because I spoke no Vietnamese.

Two days after landing by plane at the airport in Saigon, I joined my assigned infantry battalion which traveled by truck on down to My Tho. It was the first time I had ridden in a sandbagged truck with a mounted and loaded 50-caliber machine gun perched on a firing ring over the cab. The reality of war set in when the gunner locked and loaded. We began our southward journey. The clacking sound of the bolt going home made the open fields and rice paddies lining the narrow road suddenly seem very sinister.

The imagination of a green lieutenant was loosed. I pictured being ambushed, sniped at, and other assorted possibilities as we weaved through the rice paddies toward the town of My Tho.

Two of the 15-member U.S. observation team were assigned somewhere else in my battalion. I never saw them. Staff sargeant Collins, a communicator, was my companion for the first two days. Then he was assigned to the battalion's communications platoon. I was now the lone American among Asians who spoke no English.

If anything marked my observation tour to Vietnam it had to be the 1964 Christmas bombing of the Brinks Hotel in Saigon which made front-page newspapers across America. The senior American advisor of the Vietnamese Marine brigade was a Marine lieutenant colonel who happened to be staying at the hotel when it was hit. A photographer caught him rushing out the front of the hotel with only a towel on and a pistol strapped to his waist. He had been taking a shower when a truck loaded with explosives blew up in the basement. Fragments from the shower stall had shredded his skin, causing him to bleed from hundreds of tiny cuts. It was a dramatic picture that became famous in the U.S. news circles.

Viet Nam was a different kind of war. This was only the first of thousands of graphic photographs depicting our beginning involvement in what would become the longest war that America has ever fought.

Of the 15 member party of observers I went into Viet Nam with, the senior observer, Captain Cook, was hit and captured by the enemy. Another SSgt was missing in action when his unit was over run, and had to escape and evade for 15 days to avoid capture. A third observer's unit met a superior force, and he earned the Silver Star directing air strikes. My experiences in light of their experiences were uneventful.

INTO THE TEETH OF
THE DRAGON

Unknown to most of us who boarded ship that day, was the verity that we would not see our families for 13 long months, and some never again.

Marine units were formally being committed to the ground war in Vietnam. In March, two months after returning from my observation tour, my Marine unit embarked on a routine training operation in the Hawaiian Islands. Several weeks later we went ashore at Chu Lai, South Vietnam. None I knew expected it.

We were an official part of the U.S. troop buildup that didn't end for over a decade.

En route to Vietnam we stopped for several weeks in Okinawa to receive special training to prepare us for the landing at Chu Lai. However, I now know that there is little that can truly prepare a young man to take the life of another human being, especially when he comes from a country that professes to be "Christian."

Most young Americans who went to Vietnam had been exposed to God in a nominal way as kids. Most had some Christian upbringing where they heard such teachings as "thou shalt not kill," and "turn the other cheek." But few had a really solid ground or base to justify the more base (or repulsive) activities they were at times participating in. Many quickly became confused and some have stayed that way for years after the war has ended and been put behind by most Americans.

On the other hand those who had a personal relationship with God, through Jesus Christ and were committed to living in a Christian manner had a wholeness that made a real difference in how they handled themselves as combatants. Such men had fewer problems emotionally and less confusion.

Not long after arriving at Chu Lai I had the honor of participating in an event that probably seemed insignificant to some. But to Corporal Cliff Berry and interested witnesses, it was an experience that had eternal consequences. It was the day that squad leader Berry decided to be publicly baptized as a Christian. I was his platoon leader. He honored me by asking me to participate in the ritual as his sponsor.

Berry was one of those young men who had been raised in a good home. But with the threat of death more of a reality in Vietnam he was convicted he needed more of God in his life. Many downplay "foxhole conversions." But I believe God uses circumstances to bring us closer to Him. War is a good motivator. Corporal Berry made the most important decision of his life that day. He made a formal commitment to serve Jesus Christ. I was honored to be a part of it. Sadly, it was the only public baptism I saw in 27 months in Vietnam.

We had been assigned to protect the An Tan Bridge north of the Chu Lai airfield. After Cliff Berry decided to turn his life over to Christ, he sealed this decision by being baptized at the river by the bridge. So, the corporal and I, and the battalion chaplain, the Reverend John Glynn, performed this public proclamation with the dirty brown water of that Vietnamese river flowing past. Upon

the high banks over our heads were other Marines looking on. I'll never forget the silhouette high over my right
shoulder. A lone Marine sat on his guard post with an
M-14 rifle cradled in his lap, watching Corporal Berry
be buried symbolically beneath the murky waters of a
S.E. Asian river to emerge a new man in the Lord Jesus
Christ (see photo).

Some, like the corporal, gained eternally in Vietnam,
while others lost. America as a whole, well...we eventually made it impossible to win. I believe the DEROS (Date
of Estimated Return from Overseas Duty) rotation system was the beginning of the long end of our military
efforts in South Vietnam.

Christmas Eve day, 1965, a year after my wonderful
Christmas with the Vietnamese Marines, was another
memorable time for me, even though it was not as en-
joyable. My rifle company, Delta, 4th Marines, was designated as the battalion's switch company. We (the men
in my unit) were to be systematically removed and inserted into other units, and my unit would receive re-
placements with less experience and time in country. It
was mixing and matching people as if we were clothes,
or some other commodity that could be rearranged easily. But with people it isn't that easy.

In an effort to avoid having entire units rotate out of
the war zone en masse after a 13-month tour was up,
Secretary of Defense MacNamara came up with the idea
to take the existing units in Vietnam and disperse the
personnel into other units randomly so that individuals
could then rotate out without losing valuable unit battle
experience. I believe that it may have saved Department
of Defense (DOD) dollars from a material cost point of
view, but it was a monumental mistake by policy mak-
ers in terms of the added stress that it put on people.
This terrible mistake showed a gross lack of understanding of the human dynamics and such a decision could

only have been made by a person who had a very poor understanding of what motivates and makes people tick.

MacNamara recommended this idea to an inexperienced president (not a veteran) thinking that this rotation system would provide a good supply of seasoned troops always in action in the war. But it was a tragic error in presidential judgment. Four years after my first two tours we were still being impacted by that decision. Over Christmas 1968 for example, on my third tour, I lost every one of my nine rifle company squad leaders to rotation in a two-week period. I received no incoming NCOs to replace them.

Unit integrity we worked hard to achieve was totally destroyed. Instead of making the war effort more "efficient," it served to tear down the all important esprit de corps, valuable friendships, prior unit training, teamwork, and familiarity that the personnel had among themselves.

That Christmas Eve we journeyed north along the beach by amphibian tractor to DaNang. In the blink of an eye my unit, Delta company, 4th Marines, was redesignated as Delta company, 1st Bn, 3rd Marines. Their "switch" company traveled south to replace us in the 4th Marines.

In a matter of days I was the executive officer in a new company. I was too senior to be a rifle platoon commander any longer, and I spent the last three months of my second tour as a short timer among strangers.

A THIRD-TIME CHARM

In 1967, between my second and third tours, I was promoted to captain. The following year I returned to Vietnam as the commander of a rifle company. The war had intensified markedly since I had been there last. I found little to be encouraged about. The major difference between this tour and the others was the fact that I had my own rifle company. My past experience and leadership training would be put to the test. This excited me and also made me pensive. Many events of my final tour (1968-1969) in Vietnam are accentuated in my memory. But a couple of them would turn out to be highlights of my entire Marine Corps career. Certain military victories and accomplishments serve to brighten one's career. But before I share these I want to share an experience that stands out in my mind as memorable.

In 1968 my rifle company was on patrol out beyond a combat outpost called A-3. We were individually camouflaged and moving carefully on foot well spread out. The terrain was sparse and very open. I spotted three male Vietnamese dressed in black about 300 yards to the front of my point squad. I signaled for the lead squad to switch from staggered column to assault formation (on line). We continued moving forward carefully. Surprisingly, the suspected enemy troops did not see us for the longest time. By the time they did, my point squad was in a skirmish line 90 yards away. They grabbed for their weapons. My squad gunned them down. Two were killed outright. One was wounded and captured. I called for a medevac helicopter to take the wounded prisoner back for treatment and interrogation. While waiting for the chopper to arrive I personally began to examine the stout-looking young man.

While inspecting him I was aware of fear in his eyes. It was the first time in his life that he had seen Americans this close up, and he was wounded. I began checking him for hidden weapons, maps, papers, identification and noticed he was wearing a Christian cross around his neck. I reached down and lifted it up in front of his eyes and smiled at him. I then reached down inside my shirt and showed him the cross around my neck. An identifying smile brightened up his face. I saw the fear lessen with the knowledge he had something so important in common with his enemy. I offered him some water from my canteen. I also poured some of it over his head and conditionally baptized him "in the name of the Father, Son, and Holy Spirit" as I had been taught to do in case of a life-threatening injury. A few minutes later the helicopter arrived and took him away. When I later inquired I learned that the young soldier had died en route to the rear.

There is nothing like such a moment of reality experienced in war. One can learn important lessons from experiences if one takes the time to reflect back at a later date. I learned from this moment about the sovereignty of God and about how precious life really is. I know with certainty it is a benefit to be a believer no matter what side of the action you are on. This is particularly true when you are with the wrong group, as that enemy soldier was. He was a believer. On the day he met death he was blessed by the fact that he wore a cross around his neck. He could see that his enemy had an identical belief. It happened moments before he went home to be with his Lord.

OPERATION DEWEY CANYON

In the spring of 1974, five years after the most noteworthy highlight of my combat experiences in Vietnam occurred, I received a call from the public affairs office at Marine Corps headquarters. The press was taking an unusual interest in a 1969 rifle company action in which I was a principle player.

I was instructed to collect my thoughts about the episode in question and be ready to testify before a congressional subcommittee. They wanted to know why I had taken my rifle company across an international border from Vietnam into Laos in clear violation of U.S. ground combat policy.

Several days later I was shocked to see my name in a front page Washington Post news article. Major General Robert Barrow, my former regimental commander, now the commander of Parris Island, South Carolina, was also mentioned in the article. It stated that he and I would be testifying before a subcommittee of Congress.

I never testified. General Bob Barrow, in his characteristically direct manner, took full responsibility for the unauthorized border crossing. He made it very clear that if anyone was looking for a scapegoat to blame, he, as the senior tactical commander on the scene, was assuming full responsibility for all the activity regarding that operation.

The Watergate investigators were particularly interested in what my company did during this unusual action in 1969. It was speculated that they had plans for using it for political benefit years after the fact. General Barrow settled the issue satisfactorily with his testimony.

The particular rifle company action these investigators were momentarily interested in was one of several tense actions during Operation Dewey Canyon, subsequently labeled by historians a "regimental classic." In this major operation our regiment foiled North Vietnamese Army plans to aggressively push forward into the coastal regions of Hue, Quang Tri, and Dong Ha. Our eight-week-long operation resulted in a major setback for Hanoi's Communist forces. Our regiment received the U.S. Army's coveted Presidential Unit Citation, which is a rare award for a Marine unit to get.

For months our efforts up to this point had been spent searching for an elusive enemy that usually set the terms of each engagement. They chose the ground they fought on, and the time in which to strike. My involvement in

Operation Dewey Canyon was personally gratifying. We called the shots from beginning to end which was rare.

In this key operation we had the rare opportunity to go into one of the enemy's politically protected sanctuaries (Laos) to engage him on his own turf in rather impromptu fashion. For a change he had to fight on our terms.

The remoteness of the area of operations allowed the enemy no chance to turn this U.S. victory into a "press" defeat back in the States, as they did in so many other American operations. We chose this area to fight in for good reasons. One reason was that there would be no innocent civilians caught in the fighting. This eliminated Hanoi's opportunity to report so-called "war atrocities" against innocent Vietnamese people manipulated by them to the American free press. Consequently very little was heard of Dewey Canyon's success back home at the time. I take pleasure in finally filing this public report of those actions.

The major enemy resupply center for the North Vietnamese army's military operations in the northern I Corps area was the Ashau Valley. Through a series of seemingly unrelated short-duration operations over a period of months, we systematically built then abandoned fire support bases. These bases located out toward the eventual target area of operations could be easily reoccupied at any time.

In February of 1969 we swiftly reoccupied an abandoned artillery fire support base nearest the target area so we could provide artillery support for the two rifle companies chosen for the initial assault. Soon thereafter the 2nd Battalion, 9th Marines assaulted the target area.

My rifle company along with Captain Dave Buckner's were the two assault companies designated to lead the way into the area of operations (AO). We were inserted into separate locations of this very unpopulated area. Neither company met initial opposition.

During the first two weeks of the operation my company spent its time protecting and helping build a two-battery fire support base. Shortly after the initial assault the forward command post was set up at my location and Colonel Bob Barrows joined us. As commander he had better control of this bold regimental operation from this forward location.

R & R

Two weeks into the eight-week operation my R&R (rest and relaxation) rotation number came up. As I had previously arranged, I was to meet my wife in Hong Kong for five dreamed-about days. We were long overdue. It came at a pretty good time. I was able to return in time for the critical insertion into Laos with my men later on that month. We were now running local patrols protecting a fire(artillery) support base/regimental headquarters. We were on the correct side of the Vietnamese/Laotian border.

It was a hard year on me. But in light of what I now know, much harder on my spouse. Wives have it equally as rough and more so at times than many of their soldier husbands in a combat zone. They are waiting while we are on the move. With the action of combat I found plenty to occupy myself. But her routine at home was far less stimulating and slower moving. Being a "single" parent with three small children is full of stress in a different way. Time went by painstakingly slow for her. I must confess that my patience is much more severely tested when I find myself in a position of waiting for a key event to happen. Waiting can be a very hard thing to do. Many make incredibly serious life decisions by giving up too soon or simply not waiting long enough.

About the time my wife and I were beginning to let down our guard, relax, and enjoy each other again in Hong Kong, this short mini-vacation ended. The thought of the moment when we would say goodbye again was almost too painful for me. It marred the last part of my R & R leave. Soon it was time for me to return to my rifle company in the jungles of a hostile land, and for her to return to the demands of home life with small children.

OVER THE FENCE

When I got back to Vietnam after five days with my sweetheart, I experienced trouble readjusting. Emotionally and psychologically the trauma of separation from my wife and returning to combat was intense. The jump in a few short hours from the beaches and shops of Hong Kong and my wife's companionship to a rifle company on the move along the Laotian border was overwhelming. At first it was impossible for me to retain or be attentive to the new knowledge to which my platoon leaders were exposing me. I told Lt. Guins, who had been left in charge while I was away, to remain in charge for a few hours while I got back up to speed. I had to have time to collect my thoughts and do a personal regroup.

I had also experienced a problem getting back to my rifle company. The chopper in which I was traveling was nearly shot down during the approach into their position. This told me the state of the situation on the ground. It was hot! In fact four days later a medivac chopper inbound to our position to take out casualties was shot down with the four crew members on board killed. It was two days after that before we could get our casualties evacuated.

Upon rejoining my company I heard that one of the platoons had been in a firefight the day before with one Marine dead and two others wounded. The senior corpsman reported that because choppers were having a problem getting in with water, the men were showing signs of dehydration. Because of the lack of good drinking water, the rough terrain my men were working in, and the high stress level of their patrolling activities, they were suffering from advanced fatigue.

My first night back I was standing on the perimeter at a vantage point when I observed lights moving along a road in the distance. I was informed that it was Route 922 across the border in Laos. We talked about the truck lights and felt frustrated knowing that the vehicles carried Communist supplies to their army in South Vietnam. Someone said, "Wouldn't it be nice to slip down on that trail (The Ho Chi Minh Trail) and blow the dickens out of a bunch of their trucks?" Little did we know at the time that shortly we would be doing that very thing. Our pre-operation briefing had been adamant that no one was to cross the border under any circumstances.

The morning was routine. I sent out two of my infantry platoons on patrol, keeping back Lt. Guins' platoon because they had experienced a firefight the day before and were exhausted. Lt. Guin had personally chased down and tackled an NVA (North Vietnam) soldier among other things. Just before noon I received a short, coded message from battalion: "AFTER DARK, CONDUCT A COMPANY-SIZED RAID ON ROUTE 922 IN LAOS AND BE BACK ACROSS THE BORDER IN SOUTH VIETNAM BY FIRST LIGHT." My first reaction was a feeling of personal fatigue. With the senior corpsman's dehydration report still in mind, I coded a reply: "REQUEST 24-HOUR POSTPONEMENT DUE TO FATIGUE."

I knew there was a good chance that my request would be denied. I sent a message to the platoon that was working the area closest to route 922 and told them to hold up, harbor, and wait for further instructions.

I then told Al Guins, whose platoon was resting after their firefight, that if we were to make a raid that night, his platoon would be one of the two I would take. I told him we would be linking up with the harboring platoon commanded by Dick Vercautern.

The harboring platoon would be hungry so I instructed Lt. Guins to pack enough meals to feed them once we arrived at their position. Next I called the other patrolling platoon and let Lt. Pete Robertson know when he had to be back. Now I set about making essential plans for a night ambush. To this day I don't know why I figured it to be an ambush. My orders were to conduct a raid, not a night ambush.

At two o'clock in the afternoon I received a reply to my request to postpone. It was short and not so sweet: "DENIED, PROCEED."

I passed the word to my company to begin preparing in earnest.

A month previously I had received new knowledge about ambushing techniques. Because of the "denial" of my request to postpone, I felt this was an opportunity to ambush a "deliberate, known target." Otherwise why would higher headquarters not grant the delay? I inwardly felt rather certain that this was not a mere "ambush of opportunity." Certainly we would have future opportunities because we had been observing the enemy using this route the past couple of nights. They would probably be there again tonight.

I lay down to get some sleep. Darkness was only a couple of hours away. I knew that it was going to be a short night for me. My mind raced as I tried my best to fall asleep. My two-hour nap, was mingled with random thoughts flashing by.

Lt. Peterson, my other platoon commander returned with his platoon and approached me to argue passionately to allow him to go along. I explained we needed a diversion force. He was it. Purely by circumstance his was the logical platoon to provide the stay behind decoy. He was greatly disappointed.

Minus Lt. Peterson's platoon and two-thirds of my weapons platoon, we saddled up to move out late in the afternoon. My first objective was to link up with the harboring platoon and get them fed. The first leg of the patrol would be tricky business. It's always tough to link up with another friendly force in enemy territory especially if it occurs at or near dark.

Shortly after moving out I double checked to see if the extra rations were brought to feed the waiting platoon. It was a good thing that I did. First, the rations had been left behind. We stopped long enough for a fire team to go back and get them. While we were stopped, an enemy recon team happened upon our temporary position. A few bursts of fire were exchanged and the team was driven off. But most importantly we were in a static position. They had no idea we were on the move to a night ambush site.

I became concerned we would not make it to the other platoon before darkness fell. When our fire team returned with the rations I ordered a quicker pace. We linked up with the waiting platoon just before complete darkness.

In the distance we heard our stay-behind force preparing for their night defense. They were registering in their two 60 mm mortars prior to dark in case they had to fire them in defense if attacked. Four rounds exploded as they adjusted the impact area close to the perimeter.

I had instructed Lt. Peterson's platoon to man the whole company perimeter making it appear that we were all there. The enemy recon team could have been sent back to check on us again. I didn't want to tip our hand to our foes about our plans for Route 922 that night.

As the hungry platoon ate their rations and the others rested I said I would give the ambush order in 30 minutes, and took one Marine on a short recon in the direction that we would be traveling. I wanted to get a feel for the terrain prior to complete darkness.

A half hour later I returned from my short recon in total darkness. There was no moon. We were under double canopy jungle vegetation. In the darkest dark I had ever seen I issued my ambush order. Faceless leaders huddled in a tight group around the faint glow of my red-lensed flashlight. I wanted no mistakes--no accidental discharge of a weapon, no excess noise. Every man was instructed that I alone would trigger the ambush. This was made very clear. Finished, I waited for the leaders to get back to their men to issue their orders as I thought about what lay ahead. Noise discipline would be of the highest priority.

In the autumn at Quantico as a boy I remember hunting box turtles in the woods. We homed in on our unsuspecting targets by the noise they made as they walked among the dry, fallen leaves. A small, box turtle could be heard moving a hundred yards away. So I was superconscious of the noise that 85-fully-loaded men moving in the dark would be apt to make.

In those brief moments before I had them "saddle up" to move out, I prayed. I asked God to show us mercy, give us discipline, and protect us from harm. Most of all, I asked Him to silence our steps and movement.

The prayer was answered because many of us were quite awkward on this particular night. After making one stop, those in front moved out so quietly that one Marine didn't hear the man to his front leave. This created a huge gap in the column. After discovering the break I had to break radio silence to halt the front of the column. It took us 20 anxious minutes to reestablish the broken link. After that I issued the order for each man to grab hold of the entrenching tool of the man in front of him. This prevented any further breaks, but I am sure did not help us to move more quietly.

While approaching the border of the two countries we encountered another problem. The defoliant Agent Orange had been sprayed and all the leaves were dead. The defoliant's purpose was to expose enemy troop movement by making the vegetation dry and brittle which added to our noise problem.

It is a miracle we were not heard. I tried my best to keep the men quiet. But, I felt we sounded like a herd of elephants moving through thick brush.

When my lead element reached the border at the bank of the Da Krong River, they halted. This small river paralleled the road we had been sent to raid.

Moving to the point of the column, I ordered out a two-man reconnaissance of the area across the river. They would find a suitable ambush site on Route 922 in Laos.

The recon would take two hours. The rest of us settled in for the wait. It felt chilly as I cooled down from my sweaty hike. With my attention no longer zeroed in on moving troops making too much noise I lay back and looked up at the sky. To my joy I glimpsed a star through the heavy ground mist that surrounded us.

ENEMY TANK!

Minutes after Lt. Guins and Sgt. Walters had departed on their recon the sound of a powerful engine started somewhere off our left flank. The sound was unmistakable... a tank! The powerful tracked vehicle started moving in our direction. How in the world was I going to cope with a tank? The S-2 intelligence brief before this operation said nothing of enemy tank capability although I did remember that a recon unit had observed one a month back.

I had a feeling of panic as I thought about my options. Any movement we made would be chaotic, noisy, and dangerous so near R-922. I chose to remain quiet and see what developed.

Suddenly the clanking movement along the road towards us stopped. I hunkered as close to the ground as possible while waiting. Many questions and thoughts scrolled across my uneasy mind. Did they suspect our presence? I strained my eyes looking into the black Laotian night for some clue. Was that a flashlight I saw in the distance? Were they conducting a recon? My mind stopped racing in the present and took me to another raid that had taken place along the DMZ seven months earlier.

Our mission then was to create a diversion for a larger force that was sent to clear NVA (North Vietnam) soldiers out of the DMZ (demilitarized zone) who had been firing rockets into the city of Dong Ha. Then the tanks were on our side. We were riding on them.

I remember rumbling past a Chinese claymore mine that hung from a tree. Luckily it was pointed away from us. I wondered then how many we had not seen. The fleeting fear I had felt that day was nothing compared to the adrenalin pumping now.

Once you have heard a tank in motion, it's a sound you never forget. Even friendly tanks are to be feared. I thought about a training maneuver I was once on back in the States. A sleeping Marine had accidentally been killed by a tank backing over him. Since then I had developed a healthy respect for these modern day dragons of death.

The enemy tank abruptly started its engines and began moving forward again. It stopped a second time several hundred yards away from us. A powerful light flicked on and began to scan in the direction of the Vietnam border. What to do? It would reach our position in a matter of minutes. If we were discovered we would be in a vulnerable predicament. It would compromise the entire mission. I lay at the head of the column of prostrated riflemen kicking myself mentally for not having the nearest Marine cocked and ready with a light anti-tank weapon (LAW) 3.5" rocket launcher. Too late now. We were definitely not set up to engage a tank. It could spray us with deadly enfilade grazing fire. We were in no position to return effective killing fire against such a foe, a serious mistake on my part. At this point my only recourse was to trust fate. I prayed we would not be discovered.

However, my worst nightmare seemed inevitable. The tank's light flicked off again. It began to move rapidly towards us. Now it was abreast of my position and to my horror braked for its third stop right in front of me to search our position. I melted into the ground. I felt the bright searchlight rake across my back. My exposed rifle company was in the worst of all possible positions: naked, exposed and almost defenseless against a tank's fire power. Seconds seemed like minutes. What were they waiting for? Surely they saw us! When would they open fire on us?

After what seemed like an eternity the dragon released us from its grip of terror. The light went off. As quickly as the light had come upon us it was dark again. The tank revved up its roaring engine and moved noisily down the road about 1000 yards and stopped. We didn't hear it again.

How was this possible we had not been fired upon? The NVA tank crew had us dead to right. Had they really not discovered us? Questions swirled around in my dazed mind. At the same time I silently rejoiced over our good fortune. Only silent prayers could have achieved such an outcome. God had spared us.

This was nothing short of a miracle in my mind. Every Marine officer knows about tanks. Everything in the beam of that powerful search light was visible and clear to the naked eye behind the light. It was inconceivable to me that they had not spotted us at the time. As I have grown in my faith and knowledge of the workings of God, I look back and see plainly that His hand was upon every one of us that pitch black night in Laos.

AMBUSH PREPARATION

Two hours later my scouts suddenly returned to our position. They had been equally spooked by the threat of the tank. It had stopped almost directly on top of them. By scooping dirt over them in a bomb crater they remained undetected. They were so edgy after the tank left they attacked a log with their knives in the darkness thinking it was a drop-off scout.

Lt. Guins gave me his report. He reported the terrain was suitable for an ambush site. He gave me all the particulars I needed to know.

I made the decision to conduct an ambush on the Laotian side of the road facing back towards Vietnam. We could then assault through the kill zone and get back to Vietnam, facilitating our search of the area. The only problem was crossing the river located between us and the ambush site. River crossings are never fun in any kind of combat situation. It could have been particularly noisy but we crossed uneventfully.

After I and about a third of the company had crossed the road two nearby trucks started their engines and started moving towards us. They were approximately 100 yards away and I was really concerned they could hear us crossing, but I kept the men moving.

The truck's speed of travel indicated they would be upon us in about two minutes, and I was concerned they would catch us on both sides of the road. This meant we couldn't very well conduct the attack without fear of hitting our own men in the crossfire. I urged the scrambling men to double time, and passed the word for Lt. Vercautern to put his platoon in position up and to the left.

The noise of the oncoming trucks masked the sounds we were making. The last Marine came across to get into position before the first truck passed in front of me. The truck's dimmer night lights helped me see their outlines in the total darkness. The second truck passed before me. I was tempted to trigger a hasty ambush, but I was concerned about my control in the dark. I didn't want a Marine firing and hitting another Marine by mistake. The two trucks disappeared into the night. I wondered to myself if I hadn't screwed up my best chance of the night to fire up enemy supplies.

I shook it off and began to readjust the ambush force closer to the road, and posted a flank and rear guard to ensure that we had positional defense.

My two platoon commanders and I now moved forward of our defensive line of Marines and each set out a directional claymore mine. I would use my mine to initiate the ambush.

At the edge of the road where I planned to position my claymore directional mine, I suddenly found myself falling. I ended up to my armpits in a hole that seemed to have no bottom. My feet dangled in mid-air inside the hole, and with a surge of adrenaline I jerked myself free.

Intuitively I knew what it was. I had fallen into the top aperture of an enemy roadside bunker. They were used by truck drivers escaping their trucks when our air force planes bombed this part of the Ho Chi Minh Trail.

I was relieved to find this hole was unoccupied. I quickly set up my claymore near the opening of the bunker aiming it down on the adjacent road. I then carefully moved back up the hill laying out my detonation wire, and reaching my destination hooked up the wire to the triggering device.

Suddenly I had a brainstorm. I wondered out loud if anyone would like to have a ringside seat to watch the ambush materialize down front? I had never heard of posting security to the front of an ambush before, but there was always a first time and this seemed like it. I explained to those near me the benefits of having some-one down in that enemy bunker and two Marines quickly volunteered, a sergeant and a corporal.

I sent them down with a radio, a red-lensed flash-light, a LAW (light anti-tank weapon), and their personal fighting gear. They followed the det wire so they could quickly find the bunker in the darkness.

SWEATY- PALMS OPERATION

Now we settled in to wait. The ambush was set. It was 0100 hours the morning of February 22, 1969. Soon, from the west where the tracked vehicle had stopped, an occasional shot was being fired. It took me awhile to figure out what it was about, and then it dawned on me that a foot patrol was working its way back along the road occasionally reconning suspicious areas by fire. I passed the word verbally along the line that if the patrol reached our position and fired in our direction, no one was to return fire. If anyone was hit we were to remain silent.

Just short of where the tank had last checked with its searchlight the patrol turned back, and we all breathed a sigh of relief. We didn't need to skirmish with a small patrol, we were after bigger fish. At 0200 hours a single vehicle entered the kill zone and I allowed it to pass on through. Then one of my volunteers in the bunker down below broke radio silence to give a one-sentence assess-ment. He reported, "Heavily loaded six-wheeled truck with lumber sticking over the tailgate." I acknowledged by keying the radio handset.

By this one action our higher headquarters in Vietnam, who were anxiously monitoring our company net for news, finally knew that we were down on the road. Colonel Barrow would later refer to this night as his "Sweaty Palms" Operation. I had maintained radio silence since we had left our position. Our decoy stay-behind force was simulating the normal company radio traffic for us back in Vietnam.

Stillness enveloped us again and the Marines settled back and listened to crickets entertain the rest of the night creatures. Visibility improved as the ground fog evaporated, and we saw more and more stars appear overhead. It had become a fantastically beautiful night. I began to wonder exactly where I had placed that claymore mine. It was now clear where we were but down below on the road we could still see nothing. We could hear the occasional enemy voice off to the east about 900 meters, and I wondered what they were discussing. Did these people have conversations about family life, sex, love, marriage and girlfriends like us? Or were they just all business? Someday perhaps I'd know more about them.

At 0300 hours the silence was shattered by the start up of many engines all at once. They were preparing to move out. The trucks turned their blackout lights on and created a visible line several hundred yards long that turned the darkness into an eerie surreal picture of something out of a science fiction movie.

I wanted to shout at the top of my voice,*wow! Look at the size of that convoy,* but I maintained.

Obviously the convoy commander was convinced that there was no threat, and all of our scattered thoughts of being discovered were wiped away when the trucks all cranked their engines over. He had been a cautious and experienced commander and had spent much effort in trying to expose or contact us, but now he was either sure we weren't there, or the nearing daylight had forced him to make his move.

As their convoy came toward us we could see they had maintained great discipline. Their intervals were very exact, and they were coming right at us. A chance of a lifetime opportunity was crawling down the Ho Chi Minh Trail right into the teeth of our trap.

Their tight discipline posed a problem for me. Would it be possible to get two or more trucks at a time in our claymore killing zone? If not, should I hit the front of the moving convoy, the middle, or the end? I did a quick analysis of the situation and decided to hit the lead elements and hope to get any of the other trucks that we had time for.

About that time I saw one of the volunteers down at the bunker signal me with his red-lensed flashlight, as I had instructed them to do when the first vehicle entered the kill zone. I could now see the lead truck coming around the corner and as it crested the hill the driver shut down its engine and began to coast deeper into the kill zone. Then I spotted the second and third trucks following right behind.

As the second truck came abreast of me I knew it wouldn't get any better than this. At 0303 I triggered my ambush with a mighty blast from the center claymore. The truck directly in front of me immediately burst into flames and it stopped with a jerk. It was loaded with ammunition that would never be used to kill Americans in the south. Rounds began cooking off adding to the other explosions that soon filled the little valley.

The first platoon commander to my left detonated his claymore towards the lead convoy truck but it missed the cabin of the vehicle failing to stop it. The sergeant in the bunker below had been itching to do some damage anyway so he knocked out the missed target with the LAW.

The claymore to my right misfired. The third truck, its intended target, quickly began to back up out of the kill zone. Then every Marine there opened up with rifles and hand grenades. The red tracers from the American weapons lit up the darkness like the Fourth of July.

Within 30 seconds of my triggering the ambush, Lt. Tuten our forward observer had artillery falling on both of our flanks. He worked the incoming artillery rounds up and down the road to our right on which the remainder of the convoy had stopped. The artillery falling on our left discouraged that tank from getting involved in the fighting.

I now ordered my men to stand and move through the kill zone. The light from the burning truck helped me check out the area around the center truck. After five minutes I called in the flank and security elements and we proceeded back across the river and into Vietnam.

Daylight began to light up the landscape below and we could see the enemy truck drivers scurrying about to get their vehicles backed off the road and under cover, knowing they had to avoid being spotted by bombing aircraft that was sure to follow the ambush. With the new light of day coming I could also see the three disabled trucks that had entered our ambush kill zone. It was a real feeling of accomplishment.

ANOTHER NIGHT MOVE

Late that afternoon my weary Marines and I received a message to make a second night move back down to the road. We had just been resupplied by a chopper, so we used what we needed and stashed the remainder for

Fox Company who was scrambling to reach our position by nightfall.

I was bone tired, but as soon as F Company filed into our perimeter we began our second night march. It was a long night for me.

The next morning, after an exhausting and cold night march we moved into a blocking position in the same spot on the road we had been before. The heavy fog covered us as we dug in.

Not long after settling in I observed a six-man enemy patrol walking up the road toward our position. When they spotted one of my Marines a firefight broke out and we killed all of them with no casualties of our own.

The enemy had us located and were moving in mortar teams to knock us out, but my battalion commander, Lt. Colonel George Fox had heli-lifted his command post into our old position which we had left the night before upon the ridgeline. He also brought with him a 106 mm recoilless rifle that made quick work of any threat the mortar teams had in mind by knocking them all out. The enemy teams never got off a round.

SEARCH OUT AND MOP UP

During the next several days the radically changed situation caused by our crossing the border was now being taken advantage of by our company and the battalion had reinforced us.

While we began to search out and mop up the now hidden and camouflaged enemy, my point squad was ambushed as we moved up the road. They immediately took three casualties. Corporal Morgan, the squad leader singly assaulted the enemy position, which gave his remaining Marines opportunity to drag the three wounded to safety. The corporal didn't make it. In his one-man charge he was mortally wounded.

Corporal Bill Morgan, an outstanding young man, was now dead, and the words of my father rang in my head, "Today I saw the bravest man I have ever known." I began to cry with the sadness that any commander would have when he loses one of his faithful. Corporal Morgan received the Congressional Medal of Honor for the selfless act of love that he showed for his men.

The enemy ambush was trying to serve a vital purpose for the NVA. They did not want us to discover many things. First of all they didn't want us to find and capture the 122 mm howitzers, 85 mm howitzers, 12.7" anti-air weapons, all their ammunition, 12 tons of rice, and two tons of salt. But we did. We took it all! And I knew immediately what a blow we had dealt the enemy. We had won the chance game in the battle for position. Not only were they now minus some very important weaponry, but they would be forced to operate on reduced rations.

Any veteran can appreciate the exhilarating feeling that I was now experiencing. Being in a position of exploitation was almost unheard of by American forces in Vietnam. Creating havoc in the enemy's supply dump/ rear area was rare indeed for the Allies in that war, but here we were and I was loving every minute of it. My Marines were almost in ecstasy because they knew that the artillery battery we had overrun had fired many rounds against our regiment (we later learned 10,000 rounds). It was payback time for all the misery they had been causing us.

There were no longer any doubts; we had invaded a concealed NVA divisional staging area and the ambush the night before was a most timely one. In fact, that operation turned out to be the most successfully engineered ambush of the entire war in S.E. Asia, and I was honored to receive the Silver Star Medal for valor for my duty in this action.

STAND DOWN

A few days later Dewey Canyon ended for us. We were pulled out and a month later I was plucked out of my dangerous front line leadership role to another safer, cleaner position in the rear. It was a good move. I was tired and had that hollow-eyed look seen in war films. My men needed fresh leadership.

I returned to the rear, and what a change for me. I went from a shower every 4-6 weeks to the luxury of one every day. From a life of cold C-rations in the dirt and mud while on the move, I went to several hot meals a day in a dining facility. I went through a bit of culture shock, and every time I went to a movie in the evening I felt a trace of guilt thinking about the men who were still out in the boonies. I hoped they would make it back to the life they were fighting for...and certainly deserved.

SEMPER FIDELIS SUNSET

The general asked me two questions. "How long you been a company commander?" "Do you like the job?" He had been a company commander in World War II, and I'd heard that he led a company-sized raid against a small Japanese-held island in the Pacific, and won the Navy Cross for it. He held my respect as I answered his questions.

I had only been in the rear for a couple of days when I met General Jones. He wanted me as his aide, and I hadn't asked for the job. The job of aide to this great military man was a coveted position among the officers due for rotation to the rear. I knew immediately the next day after I learned of my reassignment that it was not a coincidence. God had His hand right smack in the middle of it all.

I soon learned that traveling every day with a Marine general who is in command of an infantry division can be hazardous to one's health. We spent a lot of time airborne aboard a helicopter. This aircraft has zero glide, it descends like a rock. One afternoon the chopper we were riding in suddenly quit in mid-air. Down we went. Luckily, there was a nice watery rice paddy near enough for our pilot to splash us into.

Besides the hazards, I liked being airborne with my general. At the level we flew for safety from small arms fire, it was like being in an air-conditioned building. It was a wonderful daily escape from the normal, oppressive heat that permeated unconditionally on the ground. I actually had the time to observe Vietnam from a spectator's point of view, and it was a beautiful country to fly over.

The general was a tough man, and my respect grew for him every day. A couple of months after I joined him, he took a long-range sniper bullet and only spent a few days in the hospital before he was back in the chopper visiting the troops.

I enjoyed my last four months of this third tour in combat as much as a man who misses his loved ones can. The time seemed to fly by. When I left, it was the last time I saw Vietnam, but the memories will be imbedded in my heart and mind for as long as I live.

Because of my exposure to a foreign culture and life-threatening situations, I returned to America with a more adult viewpoint of life. Prior to my initial combat experience, life was less complex. Afterwards it became more precious as my priorities had changed.

On my flight back home I had time to write and think about all three of my tours in Vietnam. The last one held its position in the forefront of my mind. I knew what had kept me safe in combat was God's mercy and love for me, the prayers of others, and my unwillingness to immerse myself in the untold numbers of sinful opportunities that were presented to all of us on a daily basis. Without a shadow of a doubt, I experienced God's mercy.

My thoughts brought me to the relationship I had with the men under my command. If there was any self-imposed letdown about my conduct as a Christian commander, it was in the area of not verbally witnessing Christ at every opportunity to each of them.

All my men respected and loved me as their leader. Most thought I was a good man. But, they did not know why I was a good man. I never told them that I was a filthy rag of a human, and if it had not have been for Christ's sacrificial crucifixion I would not have been such a "nice" guy. I didn't know how important it was at the time to share my faith with them, and now I feel sorrow for those who perished under my command without knowing about the hope of Christ.

Yes, my men thought I was a good leader, but I knew I had fallen short by not verbalizing and expressing my faith more openly. This had been a time that my faith was important to me, but I didn't realize how important it was for me to not only set a positive moral example, but to also show them the way to go spiritually.

Good moral example setting is not enough for some men, because I was their spiritual father by virtue of command. Many had come from fatherless or broken homes and I had become a substitute to not only them but to those who had fathers as well. Spiritual shyness kept me quiet as it does so many others in similar positions of authority. Even though I was happy to be getting home to my wife and the kids, these thoughts on the plane made the trip a sober one.

WELCOME TO THE WORLD

I am generally a happy, satisfied person. I trusted in God when I experienced combat fire, and I did the best I knew how when it came to dealing with the men under me. But few were saved because of my non-verbal walk with Christ. When I arrived home after this last tour I instinctively wanted more knowledge and spiritual understanding. I began to search for the "something" that I was missing, so chose to continue on with my education as a vehicle for discovery. I felt that academic courses would unlock what I needed to be spiritually complete.

After arriving home I was sent to Fort Benning, Georgia as a student to undergo a nine-month career course for senior captains and junior majors called the Infantry Officer Advanced Course. I was one of two Marine officers attending as it was an army school and army post.

It was great to be with my family, and it was also good to be tackling grades instead of enemy soldiers. One of my main goals that year was to spend as much time with my wife out on the golf course as I possibly could.

During my year at Fort Benning, the trial of Lt. William Calley was in progress on the base. It was an interesting situation to observe almost firsthand, and I concluded that Captain Medina and Lt. Calley, the defendants, must have been under tremendous stress and pressure during these trials. I only wished that I would have been presented with an opportunity or had been bolder in approaching people to share God's love with the both of them.

AIRBORNE MARINE

After my nine-month school was up I requested permission from Headquarters, Marine Corps to stay on at Fort Benning for an additional three weeks. I wanted to attend the Airborne Jump School. It was granted and I became the senior captain in the course, and subsequently was appointed the class commander.

There were 32 Marines on the course who were from forced recon at Camp Lejeune also, so I didn't feel all alone in the middle of the hundreds of army students. These tough Marines took a lot of heat making it easier for me, because the army jump master instructors loved to command a Marine officer to do pushups.

I made my first jump from an aircraft on my 31st birthday. I was now what the army called, "Airborne, all the way!" It was another school though, and I just couldn't get my fill of them. I was still looking for that "something" that was going to make the big difference in my ability to adhere to my internal moral code. Years later I finally found that "something" and it turned out to be a school that in a way I had been avoiding my entire adult life. It was a Book that I had on my list of books to read and make a part of my daily life but I had never gotten around to reading. Later it was to give me the answers that I had been searching for and a standard to hang on to when the going got rough. But that's a future story.

A HUMBLE CIVILIAN

Upon my third return from Vietnam the national scene had deteriorated tremendously. I never knew how fortunate I was to have remained in the Corps after I returned. As a careerist I returned to garrison living stateside along with other professionals preparing for the next confrontation. I had normal problems fitting back into the lives of those who had adapted to my absence, but nothing like those thousands of discharged veterans who came home and went straight to civilian life. I had some great tours: three years teaching new lieutenants at the Basic Officer School with men like Oliver L. North and "Iron Mike" Cerretta; a tour at headquarters, Marine Corps where for two years I was involved in the development of a new and more solid approach in teaching leadership training as the manager of the human relations/leadership training program for the entire Marine Corps; and a three-year tour as the Marine officer instructor at the University of Washington where I graduated from college were among the highlights. Fourteen years later, upon voluntarily leaving active duty to pursue this book, I got a taste of the huge adjustment the two-year reservists and others had made upon leaving the service.

On a particular Saturday in the spring of 1982 as a satisfied, happy career Marine everything changed for me. I was a Lt. Colonel, the inspector-instructor for the 4th Landing Support Battalion, Marine Corps Reserve, Seattle, Washington. That day I picked up the newspaper and an article motivated by the eight anniversary of the fall of Saigon smacked me directly in the face. It addressed the myriad of problems that Vietnam veterans had been suffering due to post-traumatic stress disorder. Many had lingering psychological problems since coming home from the war, and my heart was flooded with sorrow for them.

Before this I had believed that those who had not adjusted to civilian life were mostly "ten percenters" who would be a problem either in the military or out. I figured they had an inability to cope because of irresponsibility and anti-social, rebellious behavior, and that they were reaping what they had been sowing in their earlier years. In some cases this was still true but in many cases it wasn't.

How wrong I was in my general judgment! With closer inspection I found that many veterans with problems were solid citizens pulling their own weight with credible professions and jobs. All suffering from PTSD were not the long-haired drug addicts as most have been stereotyped. I also had believed that the majority who served with honor had made successful transitions and were leading normal civilian lives. I grieved that day that I had been so blind and judgmental.

I was convicted of having prejudged many of my fellow vets for not adjusting as well as I had in Vietnam's aftermath. But I saw the factor that created the major difference in their circumstance and mine. I had stayed in the service and they had gotten immediately discharged. They reentered civilian life with no real readjustment help. Their rejection was combined with a civilian culture that was out of control morally because of a changing attitude towards the use of drugs, alcohol, sex, and pornography. These factors combined with the normal pressures of living and interacting at home and work combined to throw them off guard in a manner that has now been labeled as post-traumatic stress disorder (PTSD). They seemed to have no answers. I had been sheltered by the military umbrella, and didn't realize what the other side of the coin looked like until I too left the military as a retiree. It has been a difficult readjustment for me, even after so many years of military covering.

In 1982 a very simple truth came to me. Many men having problems adjusting to civilian life had been responsible as military men in a duty sense and they had no clue to the root of their present day problems. I knew at that moment why I had had some unusual experiences both in and out of the formal classroom. A deep desire was birthed in me to help veterans adjust to civilian life, and to encourage those still on active duty. That same day I began writing a book of which this book is a part. One year later I made a soul-wrenching decision to leave the Marine Corps to devote full time to this project. I left the military with a heart full of memories and a head full of ideas. As I look back now over the past thirteen years, I see that I was often derailed, and at times the project seemed to have died a natural death. But I have never given up hope that one day I would have a real opportunity to begin to make a difference in the lives of my generation, and in the lives of the sons and daughters of those who so faithfully answered the call to arms in Vietnam. With God's help I will see my 1982 vision fulfilled.

Many of my prayers since leaving the Corps have been for the future of our military, and for the young men and women who are now serving faithfully to preserve a strong America. I hope that our sons and daughters will never see the same conditions to which the Vietnam veterans returned. But knowing the folly of human nature, I felt it important to offer encouragement from my lessons learned in the form of this book. It has been forged from my experiences. From the moment I read the suicide statistics among Vietnam veterans in 1982 (many more killed themselves after returning home than were killed at enemy hands in the war), I knew that I had to leave something really tangible so that the next generation would be better off for our negative experiences than were we who lived through them.

Part II of this book is my contribution to that cause.

Grandfather Winecoff (second row, right) displaying his riding skills on the University of Georgia's trick riding team.

55

Chinese Emperor, Chang Kai Shek decorating Dave's
father (1/5 Marine Battalion Cmdr.) in 1946

Dave's father (far left) in 1950, attending
Chesty Puller's promotion celebration.

Famous retreat from the Chosen Resevoir (1st Marine Division) — Dec 1950. Dave's father wrote the plan for the division's withdrawal.

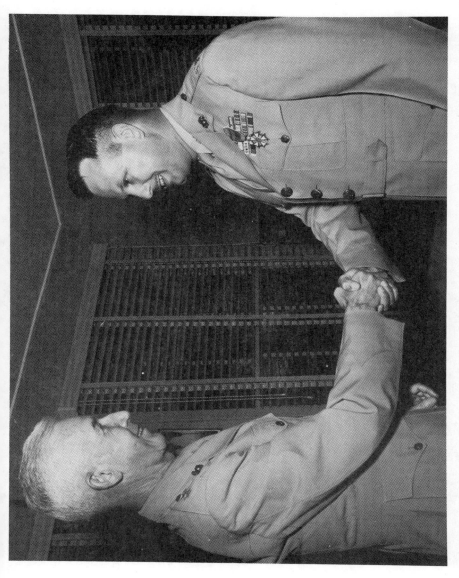

1951 — Gen. O.P. Smith decorating Dave's father for action in Korea.

1951 — Dave's dad, the Colonel.

Dave (far right) graduating sixth grade at Camp
Pendleton, 1952, with Gen. O.P. Smith , Colonel Price
and two fellow student class leaders.

1956 — Dave as a sophomore on the high school track
team, Quantico, VA.

Dave receiving outstanding senior ROTC award in college in 1962.

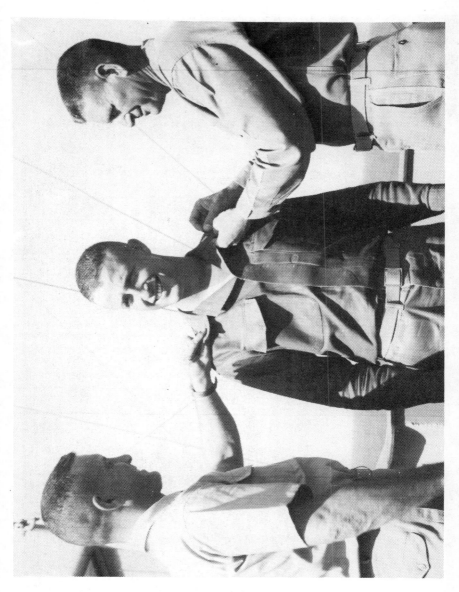

Dave's shipboard promotion to 1st Lt. 1964 (left) Capt.
Bob Philon, (right) Lt. Col. A.I. Thomas.

Dave and Bob Johnston on hike break, Oahu, Hawaii—1963. Lt. Gen. Johnston was Commanding General of Somalia Expedition and Executive Officer of Desert Storm.

65

Father and daughter, Mary, just before dad (Dave) left
for Vietnam in 1964.

DaNang, South Vietnam in 1964. The captain sitting
was captured by the enemy and was one of the
P.O.W.s unaccounted for.

Dave participating in a combat zone baptism along the
banks of a Vietnamese river — 1965.

Mortar pit chapel—Lt. Cmdr. William Childers holds a
service for the Ninth Marines near the Laotian border.

2/9s Company Commanders—Captain Ward, Sutten, Henselberger, and Winecoff.

Left to right—Al Guins, Dick Vercautern, Dave.

L to R — Dave Slaigle, Dave, Al Guins, Jack Cyr (lower)
John Guiligo, "Pete" Petterson, SSGT Perez.

Dave's autographed photo of his Senior Commanding
General, R.G. Stilwell (CG, XXIV Corp, Vietnam who
commanded Ray Davis' 3rd Marine Division)

Dave and other senior officers appearing at a special services day held by the Seattle Mariner's baseball team.

Dave christens the new Marine obstacle course used in
the film, "An Officer and a Gentleman," Sand Point
Naval Station, Seattle—1982.

Colonel Dave's children:
L to R — Mark, Mary, Steve, Scott

Part Two

Survival Depends on the Life Value You Choose

DESTINY'S CALL

America's Secret Weapon

"Faith is confident assurance concerning what we hope for, and conviction about things we do not see. Through faith we perceive that what is visible came into being through the invisible by faith."
Hebrews 11:1

Boys dream of and act out in their play the role of fictional super-heroes like Superman, Batman, or Tarzan. Where their youthly idealism develops into a strong, healthy faith they come to admire real-life heroes of destiny like the two men highlighted in this chapter. The tragedy is that idealism in so many of our young is so soon dampened, tarnished, or discarded just when they are being challenged to show increased responsibility. Few seem to follow through with their idealistic boyhood dreams. Unselfish greatness is an increasingly rare thing. So our society is in growing trouble. In a survey we find the desire bloomed in leaders to become a Marine (a sacrificial lifestyle) most often around the eighth grade.

Famous men of destiny who have left their mark on history are men of vision and faith. What makes them uncommon is that they have not compromised the virtues that other men identify with and find attractive: trustworthiness, loyalty, bravery, reverence. Their internal moral code in important key areas is still functioning as adults. They have a clear vision of what they want to accomplish. We of lesser stature can identify with their strong character as we are all called to grow in the direction of a stronger set of morals.

A TALE OF TWO MARINES

We all profit from getting to know better the background, character, and accomplishments of real heroes like my two favorite historical Marines. Both had uncommon faith, though their faith appears to some to be anchored on two different foundations. Major General John A. Lejeune, America's thirteenth Commandant of Marines, was a man's man, as was his most famous prodigy, the Marine Corps' man of mystery, Lt. Colonel Pete Ellis.

John Lejeune, who was born just before the start of the Civil War saw his first Marine when his father took his young sons to visit a naval ship on display in Charleston harbor. When young John saw the handsome Marine officer of the day in his colorful dress uniform at the top of the gangway, then and there he decided one day he too would be a Marine officer. His fancy was captured at the height of his youthful idealism. That idealism never waned. John Lejeune had a distinguished 39-year career. Following retirement he went on to lead a fruitful civilian life. He died after my birth, and well before I had any inkling of such a career myself. Only later did I become interested in the deep motivation behind his long years of accomplishment.

Career Marines will tell you John Lejeune's spirit of service and sacrifice lives on in the Corps. This is my belief too. His original birthday message, founding the annual birthday celebration, is reread to Marines around the Corps before the cutting of the cake on November 10th. This is one of several key programs he initiated which are still in effect. His first message continues to inspire all Marines. I never tire hearing it.

When I think of Lejeune I think of leadership and of his most famous prodigy, the mystery man, Lt. Colonel Pete Ellis, the father of modern amphibious warfare.

Marines usually have one or two leaders they admire intensely and some they dislike just as intensely. While I was a Basic School instructor, (1970-73) I read and analyzed two pages on leadership in the Marine Corps manual for the first time that I now recall (though I am sure I must have been exposed to it as a student lieutenant). General Lejeune's words on leadership are classic. They caused a desire in me to want to become better acquainted with this long buried Marine. His annual birthday message had thrilled me on a half dozen occasions by the time I had assumed my Basic School duties. As a tactics instructor in the patrolling department, Oli North became one of my everyday cronies. At that time Lejeune's written words in the manual had remained untouched by revisionists for over half a century, quite a testimony to their power. Bureaucrats in headquarters love tampering with words in perennial documents. Legend has it these treasured words on leadership were actually coined by Lt. Colonel Pete Ellis with guidance and final editing by Commandant Lejeune.

THE AGE OF HEROES

Many say the "Age of Heroes" is over. Critics relish parading discovered faults of well known historical figures thereby mocking their historical accomplishments as luck. Lejeune, like all men, had shortcomings. It is a leader's vision, moral strength and spirit of sacrifice that cause men to willingly follow, not his weaknesses which most men are generous enough to overlook. Strength propels leaders into the ranks of the great men of history. Weakness only defeats a leader when it degenerates into folly, overriding his virtues to cloud his judgment. Professional critics are paid to point out weakness. But the majority of men attracted to greatness mercifully overlook weakness because of the compelling nature of vision and commitment.

The historical accomplishments of these two have stood the test of time. John Lejeune's character compared with that of Ellis is treated more reverently, but I don't think it is because of their difference in rank or sacrifice. Ellis paid a dear price for his historical achievement: an early, tragic death. In my view this can be traced to a major mistake in judgment resulting from a wrong underlying assumption. The assumption upon which a leader's decisions rest are critical. Too often wonderfully talented men and women are crippled by faulty assumptions.

What we learn from studying these two famous Marines is revealing. I will address key principles of life over the next five chapters as we study the formation of enduring character in the light of these two men of destiny. Both left a lasting legacy to the Corps and nation. Ellis is virtually unknown today outside of knowledgeable Navy-Marine Corps historical circles while Lejeune's name is widely revered. The largest concentration of

Marines in America is at Camp Lejeune, North Carolina. Lejeune started the Corps modern day educational system. Marines and their guests hear his birthday message reread annually. His biggest accomplishment may have been the fact that after four decades of difficult family life with frequent separations and hardship he still enjoyed the love, respect and devotion of his family. He enjoyed many years into retirement the love of a wife and three daughters.

THE UNPREDICTABLE
LIEUTENANT COLONEL

Within the Corps there is a small number of die-hard Marines "Who run rather curiously to type" as John Thomason, a Marine and WW I author wrote long ago. Lt. Colonel Pete Ellis was certainly one of these "lifers" distinguished by his total commitment to the Corps. Lt. Col. Ellis was a man of passion, devoted to the profession of arms. He was very good at what he did. Such men still exist today. The country is better off because of their presence. The country was exposed to one of these men, Oli North, during the Iran- Contra trial.

Pete Ellis had a brilliant mind, boundless energy and a driving spirit of purpose. He was an adventurer at heart. Quite early in his career he attracted the notice of frontrunners while on a tour in the Philippines, among them a future commandant John Lejeune, then a major.

While in the Philippines on his first duty assignment as an officer, Ellis had a run in with the brigade chaplain. This provides a clue about his spiritual and moral bent.

He lived off base with two Marine officers in native territory. One day the brigade chaplain dropped by unexpectedly and was invited to stay for dinner. What followed was recalled by a friend of Ellis and recorded in Lejeune's book.

"The chaplain's overly righteous attitude discouraged any kind of rapport. A few drinks and stories before dinner only worsened matters. After the four had eaten in silence and were waiting for the houseboy to remove the plates, Ellis apparently found the situation too oppressive. He whipped out his revolver and shot the plates off the table."

Pete had joined the Corps in 1900 as a private from Pratt, Kansas. He graduated number one academically from his high school at a time when the Marines had very few high school graduates. Just past the age of twenty-one he was offered and accepted a commission as a second lieutenant.

A significant part of his career was to be spent in the Pacific Ocean area. He had a questioning, analytical mind and tackled the challenge of learning the Japanese language. He was comfortable living outside the familiarity of overseas military compounds.

Early in his career he became suspicious and distrustful of the future intentions of the Japanese and became bolder and bolder in sharing his personal convictions. He earned noteworthy adherents through the force of his intellect, such as the now famous naval officer, Admiral Sims. During a naval war college tour as an instructor he won key future admirals and generals to his theory concerning the future.

Ellis spent more time beyond the border of the U.S. than at home during his career. At the start of WW I he personally traveled to the war zone with General Lejeune serving as the Marine Brigade's adjutant in Europe. In this capacity he distinguished himself in such a superior fashion that he was awarded a Navy Cross for excellence in staff work, an unheard of justification for combat valor.

Among other notable accomplishments he prepared a plan for an assault by Lejeune's division resulting in a penetration of the entire German defensive position forcing the enemy to withdraw thirty kilometers. This was called the "greatest single achievement of the 1918 Campaign." Lejeune was promoted up from the Marine Brigade to C.O. of the division shortly before the attack. General Lejeune was one of two Marines to ever be trusted with leading an army division in combat.

Following WW I, Ellis' personal views landed him frequently in hot water. He was finally muzzled after an impromptu speech where a reporter who happened to be present in the audience dutifully reported his remarks.

DAYS OF ISOLATION

Our nation slipped into an isolationist, anti-naval attitude following WW I. His particular point of view concerning a future Japanese threat was not popular with a sitting congress until after the Pearl Harbor attack December 7, 1941. Few were as vocal as Ellis. It was popular to be a pacifist after WW I. Most military experts were mired in academic mud analyzing the largely trench warfare of that European war. Ellis held radically different ideas of the threat lying in America's future. He disagreed with most European historians of that era. His views later proved prophetic. He was a visionary, out of tune with the standard wisdom of his day. Had not John Lejeune while commandant reached down elevating Ellis at a critical moment in history, at the very least WW II would have been twice as long with millions more dying.

Educators across our country are currently taking this generation of Americans in what they sincerely believe is a sane direction to achieve peace at any cost. I see our age as equally dangerous as was the "anti-naval" period of the 1920s. The heralded ending of our Cold War with Russia has given civilians a false sense of security. Human nature today is not more civilized than before. Will we repeat the mistakes made by our predecessors between WW I and WW II as a body? Or will a small group of realists help prepare us for another coming time of great challenge? (see "George Washington's Prophesy" in References)

As you will see, God clearly used the talents of Lt. Col. Pete Ellis in the early 1900s assisted by the mentoring actions of General Lejeune to prepare America for final victory over our adversaries 20 years later.

Joseph Addison in the August 16, 1712 *Spectator* said:

"A person may be qualified to do greater good to mankind and become more beneficial to the world, by morality without faith than by faith without morality."

RELATIONSHIP IS THE KEY

Relationships are an important key in unlocking the riddles of life. Neither Ellis or Lejeune would have been as successful without the other. History proves there was an adequate measure of 'faith' and 'morality' available through the joint efforts from the most dynamic duo of the pre-WW II era.

The prodigious academic feat for which Ellis has been given the title, "Father of Amphibious Warfare" took place at Headquarters, Marine Corps. He was ordered there, one of Lejeune's first acts after becoming the commandant in 1920. He was given a private office and a typewriter. For three months nearly around the clock, Ellis put his convictions and observations into a comprehensive report interrupted occasionally by several forced rests in the hospital. The final result of this intense blitz was a 30,000-word study labeled, "Advanced Base Operations in Micronesia." This top-secret operation plan was approved by the commandant on July 25, 1921.

I have read everything Ellis wrote that I could discover through my research. Several articles published about him make direct reference to his alcoholic, sometimes amoral behavior. He definitely had a worldly wild streak. He was called on the carpet by his seniors for after hours excesses on several occasions. But in spite of this obvious character defect his deep devotion to Corps and country overshadowed his ego -generated problems. He is remembered historically as one who clearly laid down his life for his country.

From a medical point of view, Ellis' personal and physical needs near the end of his life were great. His health deteriorated rapidly during his spying mission. Modern day doctors of medicine analyzing his extensive medical record would have advised the commandant against allowing him to have his requested two-year leave of absence. But he was discharged to go secretly investigate what the Japanese Empire was up to. In hindsight, by carrying through with this bold plan of action, his death was certain. Ellis distrusted the politics in play in his day and had hidden his plans from the State Department.

He left with General Lejeune's apparent permission on his ill-fated spying trip. In the guise of a civilian trader he roamed the Pacific Ocean area under the control of the Japanese.

Intellectually, he had the skills required to succeed. Physically, he was debilitated. He proved to be a brave, but spiritually reckless man. Deep down he suspected the outcome might prove fatal for him. He told his family not to look for him, and that he might never see them again.

Ellis' medical record shows a series of hospital visits and stays that progressively increased. He checked into overseas naval facilities twice for hospitalization during his abortive mission. He had a nervous condition usually brought on by overwork called: "neurasthenia" or "psychothenia." He would become nervous, tense, and emotionally unstable. His hands would tremble. He had major attacks of insomnia and hyperactivity and battled bouts of depression.

From what is recorded of the Marine Corps' official investigation into his death following the end of WW II in 1946, his eternal destiny does not appear promising. The report turned up a non-Japanese eyewitness of his death back in 1922. This witness said his final hours were spent in a drunken madness. In rage in the bitterness of despair he threw every item including furniture out of the window of the house he had rented on the Japanese-controlled island. He died later that night.

On island after island Ellis was unable to find the bunkered, dug-in defenses he had clearly pictured in his mind's eye, and had been preaching about for years. These defenses were built only years after his death. He obviously found this discovery terribly depressing. He had clearly envisioned these defenses as they occured exactly twenty years later.

DEATH OF A VISIONARY

In May, 1923 Ellis' mysterious death was reported in the *New York Times* as a lead story. The Japanese sent his cremated body back to the U.S. in an urn. The paper wanted to know what this highly vocal Marine officer was doing wandering around the Pacific Ocean posing as an American trader? The commandant stonewalled. He was ultimately forced by the sensitivity of his high office to disassociate himself officially from Ellis. The political explosiveness of being linked directly with a man the press was attacking as a jingoist was too risky for the office he held. In 1924 Ellis' administrative work became the basis for a top secret Army-Navy effort at the War Department known as the "Orange Plan" in the event of future war with Japan.

Officially, Ellis was reported as absent over leave. However, it was known by his close friends that Ellis had officially called on the commandant the day before his departure. He had been observed handing over to the commandant a white envelope which Lejeune put in his desk drawer without looking at it. Speculation has it that this was an undated official letter of resignation from Ellis in case he was caught by the Japanese and became a liability to the country. Lejeune never used this letter. Later he apparently destroyed it.

FORCED-ENTRY TECHNIQUE

Ellis' effort proved an amazingly prophetic insight into events 20 years into the future. He predicted with uncanny accuracy enemy actions and allied counter-actions that later occurred. He identified in great detail the future threat the Japanese Empire would become to the U.S. and the world. He laid out in painstaking fashion revolutionary tactical concepts and future requirements which today stand as a brilliant reminder of his genius and foresight.

His estimates, such as the number of assault troops (4,000) required to penetrate the defenses of the Japanese on Eniwetok in the Marshalls were mind-shattering in their accuracy. Almost the exact number were used in the penetration of that atoll in 1944.

This prophetic document became the cornerstone which his disciples used to launch a quietly intense, 20-year effort to restructure the Navy-Marine Corps team just before a time of critical need. By the end of WW II thanks to this critical effort the Marine Corps was able to expand thirty times their pre-Pearl Harbor strength. The doctrine of the "forced entry" technique needed according to Ellis to defeat the Japanese was later taught to the army by special teams of instructors from the Marine Corps. The army learned from the Navy-Marine Corps team how to plan for and conduct amphibious operations. These operations were later used brilliantly by army general, Douglas MacArthur in the southern Pacific and to penetrate fortress Europe from the sea. The Ellis doctrine explained why Marines were so awesome in Pacific Ocean assaults on seemingly impregnable Japanese strongholds.

The Japanese Admiral in charge of the defense of Tarawa was quoted as saying before the assault, "A million U.S. Marines couldn't capture this island in a thousand years." Tarawa fell in a matter of days. Without Ellis' early boldness (he was clearly not part of the crowd of pacifists) the Japanese admiral would not have been far off the mark.

His pioneer work gave us the techniques and tactics at the start of our offensive counterattack in 1942 to accomplish what we achieved at Guadacanal and in subsequent island-smashing operations. We could not have forced our way onto the hostile German-controlled European or African continents. We could not have captured the strategic islands in the Pacific without the sacrifice of a Pete Ellis or the confidence in his subordinate of a John Lejeune. God stirs men anew in similar ways in every generation.

The only other forced entry technique that had been developed prior to WW II was the strategic drop of airborne battalions behind enemy lines. The U.S. Army's assault against the German-held shores of France proved that this technique couldn't crack a tough nut. Those army battalions that were dropped behind the German beach defenses at Normandy received 90-100 percent casualties in a matter of hours and wouldn't have survived without the reinforcing beach landings.

THE MATCH AND THE FLAME

Lt. Colonel Pete Ellis, a religious skeptic, was the vital catalyst God used to prepare America in time to defeat the German and Japanese attempt to divide up the world between them. General Lejeune was the match God used to light aflame his prodigy, Pete Ellis. This potent pair is the key dynamic duo behind military success in WW II.

Ellis' concepts were tested in once yearly practice landings by the navy and Marines. They got the chance to prove these theories worked under fire when they were given the go-ahead nod to conduct the first offensive action of WW II, the Guadacanal landing and campaign. My dad participated in this initial nine-month long campaign. He also participated in several in the middle, and the last one to end the war in the Pacific, the bloody battle for Okinawa.

Ellis' death galvanized others into a quietly, persistent 20-year effort. The result? America prevailed in WW II. I need to point out the disastrous failure of the Allied amphibious attempt at Gallipoli in 1917 conceived by Churchill. Few experts had confidence in any ability to prevail from the sea against a strong land defense. Yet, God ensured that the Nazi and Japanese effort in WW II would fall short. Ellis pioneered the plan to ensure this most complex of all attack techniques would later work by following his perceived path of destiny.

It is interesting Lejeune in his memoir published ten years after Ellis's death and ten years before the start of WW II refered to Ellis nine times throughout his book. He did so in a most casual manner. Of course he could not mention the top-secret war plan, nor did he refer to the mysterious death of Ellis. The off-handed manner in which he made reference to Ellis is especially intriguing. Ellis' secret work was classified at the time of the publication of Lejeune's memoirs. Ellis name was mentioned more than the name of any other Marine's, quite a compliment.

A desire to say something positive about Lt. Colonel Ellis following his death had to be a prime motivation for General Lejeune's writing of his classic book (see reference section). The women in Lejeune's life: his wife, sister, and three daughters prodded and pushed him in a loving way to write his memoirs. His love for his prodigy, the deceased Lt. Col Ellis, explains to me why his book places such a powerful emphasis on the moral and spiritual values that undergirded his style of leadership. For the generation in which he lived, his writing is very spiritually bold. He points the way for future Marines to the importance of lifestyle in achieving destiny.

THE ANNUAL BIRTHDAY MESSAGE

Before I ever knew Lejeune had written a book, I was struck to the heart by the force of two of his writings, his annual birthday message and the two pages on the subject of leadership in the Marine Corps Manual. An extract from the manual is worthy our attention:

> Teacher and scholar - The relation between officers and enlisted men should in no sense be that of superior and inferior nor that of master and servant, but rather that of teacher and scholar. In fact, it should partake of the nature of the relation between a good father and his son to the extent that officers, especially commanding officers, are responsible for the physical, mental, and moral welfare, as well

as the discipline and military training of the young men under their command who are serving the nation in the Marine Corps. The realization of this responsibility on the part of officers is vital to the well-being of the Marine Corps. It is especially so, for the reason that so large a portion of the men enlisting are under twenty-one years of age. These men are in the formative period of their lives, and officers owe it to them, to their parents, and to the nation, that when discharged from the service they should be far better men physically, mentally, and morally than they were when enlisted.

A leader's moral makeup affects all outcomes. The process by which a leader reaches decisions is vital. It often explains the whys of victory or defeat. Leaders who brilliantly brainstorm the best possible course of action while ignoring the spiritual dimension set aside a precious insight.

When I discovered Lejeune's written memoir in the Camp Lejeune library while on a staff trip from HQMC in 1974, I immediately adopted him as a spiritual father/hero. I had no idea this wonderful book was still available in print through the Marine Corps Gazette's bookstore. For me there was a deep inspiration in his writings. Surely he was God's man on the scene during a critical moment in history.

Few aware citizens today would disagree that immorality has a terrifying grip on the destiny of America. The impact that hedonism has on our civilian population and its effect on the morality of soldiers, sailors, airmen, coast guardsmen and Marines is profoundly disturbing. Our ability to defend this nation is eroded as our collective ability to sacrifice for the common good declines. This erosion as evidenced so graphically by Pete Ellis, declines with the increasing centeredness on self. Today we live among skeptics, critics, and worse. I like what General Shoup, friend of my dad and former Marine Corps Commandant, had to say about critics.

"The galleries are full of critics. They play no ball. They fight no fights. They make no mistakes because they attempt nothing. Down in the arena are the doers. They make mistakes because they try many things. The man who makes no mistakes lacks boldness and the spirit of adventure. He is the one who never tries anything. He is the break on the wheel of progress. And yet it cannot be truly said he makes no mistakes, because his biggest mistake is the very fact that he tries nothing, except criticizes those who do things."

LETTERS FROM A HERO

No one knows the true state of the heart of a man except his Maker, and if the man is honest, he has much more reason to learn what God thinks of him. I just want to pick a few quotes from John Lejeune's memoirs to give you insight into why I admire this man the way I do. He wrote home in letters to his wife very insightful thoughts. She saved the letters and they have become the source for parts of his book. Lejeune said:

> There is no substitute for the spiritual, in war. Miracles must be wrought if victories are to be won, and to work miracles men's hearts must needs be afire with self sacrificing love for each other, for their units, for their division, and for their country. If each man knows that all the officers and men in his division are animated with the same fiery zeal as he himself feels, unquenchable courage and un-

conquerable determination crush out fear, and death becomes preferable to defeat or dishonor. Fortunate indeed is the leader who commands such men. And it is his most sacred duty to purify his own soul and to cast out from it all unworthy motives, for men are quick to detect pretense or insincerity in their leaders, and worse than useless as a leader is the man in whom they find evidences of hypocrisy or undue timidity, or whose acts do not square with his words. To be a really successful leader, a senior officer must avoid aloofness, too he should not place himself on a pedestal and exercise command from a position far above the heads of his men, but he must come down to the ground where they are struggling and mingle with them as a friend and as a father.

From another letter to his wife this pearl was picked:

In war, if a man is to keep his sanity, he must come to regard death as being just as normal as life and hold himself always in readiness, mentally and spiritually, to answer the call of the grim reaper whenever fate decrees that his hour has struck. It is only by means of this state of mind and soul that a man can devote all his thoughts, all his intellect, and all his will to the execution of the task confided to him. Personal fear paralyzes all the faculties, and the attributes of first importance in a commander is freedom from its cold and clammy clutch. Fortunately, a normal man is so constituted that his mind refuses to dwell on morbid ideas, but is ever buoyant, active, and intent on performing the duties assigned him. His thoughts, therefore, turn constantly to the future and do not dwell on the tragedies, the suffering, or the horror of the past. While war is terribly destructive, monstrously cruel, and horrible beyond expression, it nevertheless causes the divine spark in men to glow, to kindle, and to burst into living flame, and enables them to attain heights of devotion to duty, sheer heroism, and sublime unselfishness that in all probability they would never have reached in the prosecution of peaceful pursuits. Thousands, aye millions of the men who have engaged in war have shown themselves to be truly the children of God.

In another letter his spiritual character shines. "...At 5:30 a.m.the infantry attacks. We have a great task ahead of us and a fight that will try men's souls. I pray God that we may win, and end this horrible war by a decisive victory. Many a poor fellow will give his life to his country tomorrow. The men are brave, strong, and determined to beat the enemy. I believe that God will give me the strength to go through the ordeal which is before me. I shall ask his blessing and his assistance before I lie down tonight."

The next writing shows his understanding of the sovereignty of God.

"It is a solemn time just before a battle, but it is as if one were in the hands of fate. We do not enter into battle of our own accord. It is always someone in higher authority who gives the order. In our case, it emanates from Marshal Foch, but he is only the servant of the nations allied against the common enemy. One grows to feel that God speaks through the peoples of the world, and that in some inscrutable way it is his command that we fight to the death."

General Black Jack Pershing, A.E.F. (commander, American Expeditionary Force) later said of this battle: "...His division was directed with such sound military judgment that it broke and held, by the vigor and speed of its attacks enemy lines which had been considered impregnable."

THE DYNAMIC DUO

I believe these two great men of destiny were the dynamic duo that prepared us to win WW II against dictatorial Japanese and German regimes of that day. The development of the revolutionary new amphibious assault techniques allowed us to storm ashore against their strongholds, and withstand their formidable military machinery, will power, and counter attacks. This victory came at great cost due to the initial direction and belief of the majority in our democratic society who were largely blind to the coming collision of lifestyles.

The failure of the Allied amphibious attempt at Gallipoli to end the First World War was a bitter disappointment for Churchill. It was a nine-month struggle ending in failure. Subsequently none of the world's experts believed an army could land from the sea against a well established land force and prevail. The vision of Pete Ellis, the faith and wisdom of John Lejeune and the follow through of a small band of Ellis' disciples during an isolationist and pacifistic period much like today changed military skepticism. The United States proved ready to take on and defeat two formidable totalitarian regimes both bent on world conquest at the same time.

The popular experts of the day were terribly wrong in their prediction of the future. We all hope for world peace. But what does history have to say about the possibility of the same thing happening again? Is human nature different now? Can world leaders or the United Nations really be trusted, no matter how sincere they might be? Are we seeing the disarming and turn over, bit by bit, of United States sovereignty to a United Nations whose hopes are based on false expectations by a powerful elite? Is the political change in the former Soviet Union really permanent? Decentralized Communist power has been put into the hands of the Soviet republics. Can this power be reconsolidated under a hardliner in the future?

Right now men are needed whose vision of the future is unpopular, to prepare our people to cope with quite a different future from the one being projected by the prevailing media opinion. Hope is good but it can't be anchored to false beliefs. Blind trust in what other countries leaders say should not guide our national security decisions. We must base our national defense on what the capabilities of a coalition of nations are if they were to align against us militarily.

The majority of Americans will continue to take the easy path of least resistance. It's human nature. God always challenges a remnant with a vision of a different future so that His people are well led when the unexpected comes. The narrow path seems at the time very difficult. But there is great reward later on for those who follow it. Destiny means following one's heart instead of only one's head. Most behave in a manner consistent with their basic underlying assumptions concerning the nature of man. Let us now look at that nature more closely.

THE MAKING OF A MAN

"Be on the alert, stand firm in the faith, act like men..."
1 Corinthians 16:13

What is the correct path to mature manhood? We all start out wanting to make a difference in life. Why do so many fall away from their initial, idealistic aims? The prevailing wisdom of our modern world says old images of manhood are worn out. A new and different standard is needed. Today's male, if he holds to traditional values, needs in feminine terminology a "makeover." The many contradictions that riddle our society ensure that those who haven't had the benefit of strong parenting will have a distorted image of genuine manhood. As American men, we need to refocus.

The first half of this book dealt with waging war. Let's look now at the subject of masculinity more closely. Males who desire to become real men need to reach by the age of 18 (legal responsibility), some worthwhile conclusions about the path this development needs to take. The generation now assuming leadership needs to have its collective "act" together because of serious problems they face. Future generations will prove even more confused about their manhood than many of today's males if today's leaders don't make positive changes. Those demonstrating their mental confusion through increasingly feminine dress and jewelry standards, need real help.

Two decades associated with the Marines who stress manliness, strength, courage, endurance, dependability and discipline (all very useful in overcoming evil) give me a clear perspective on the topic of manliness. I have seen men at their best. I have seen them at their worst in combat, the most difficult of environments. Crisis experiences give me a sound platform from which to comment on my observations of men and their behavior.

TRUE MASCULINITY

Masculinity, contrary to what the youth culture says, is not rooted in the conquering of a woman. It can only come from conquering a man. Not conquering another man as in war, but one's self. Many men I've known have worked hard at self conquest. Those who let down their moral guard become corrupt over time, losing self-control in critical arenas. When men lose their self-control they squander, little by little, their morals in a world all too willing to consume them.

A Christian man should have a pretty good understanding that he can't overcome himself through mere human effort (Romans 7:18). But our nation is full of men raised on the entertainment industry who have received a false message. It is not surprising how little difference there is in the actions of Christians and non-Christians today because of the permissive culture in which we grow up.

Men have become more confused about true masculinity in the wake of the sexual revolution with angry women demanding their "sexual liberty." Wining and dining a woman for the purpose of securing sexual favors is a dangerous business. Many have informally been taught to play this game. They are easy prey to lawsuits and condemnation. The use of money, superior power, and position for leverage in this stupid game is costing society plenty these days. The prevailing culture teaches that women can be skillfully deceived to get them to go along with the sexual program. Alcohol, money, drugs, and food are all lures to effect the "conquest." There is still a locker room mentality where boasting is made by both men and women of conquests along the passage to adulthood. The male who wants to be a virgin at the time of marriage (I was one of those men) is somehow made to think of himself as less than a man. With age and maturity, intelligent men learn such tactics backfire. The case of the young Marine on the embassy security force in Moscow is a classic example of the bad things that result. His lack of self-control got him entangled with a female Russian spy and eventual court martial.

By the age of 40 it is clear to most men that locker room concepts of manhood learned as a boy don't hold much water. So what does this discovery do? Where does one go with this revelation? Are our sons going to learn anything different? What are the attributes of a real man?

THE WARRIOR IMAGE

The world of advertising dictates a radically different model for the 1990s male than the 40-year old knows has been effective for him. Yet most of us have been brainwashed and few know what's really missing. Traditionally, men were taught that physical strength and silent patience were the main ingredients needed for success in life.

Most of us grew up with this model: suppress pain, be aggressive, don't whimper or complain, be steady, strong and a good provider. Somewhere along the way we learned not to fall victim to the emotional whims of women. We thought strength, silence and decisiveness were the keys to effectiveness in life. Men who appear to have all these attributes on the outside, may inside feel deprived, confused and passive. Such men don't really fit in anymore.

As the women's liberation movement gained momentum, "soft" men were the types these women exalted. From the 1960s on a new man began emerging that opposed the venerable, traditional "model" of the 1950s. But has the soft, gentle man that emerged from the "love and peace generation" been the answer frustrated women wanted? Because of their continued and increased frustration, it seems not.

Most of us remember the 60s. This new "free" man was anti-establishment. He confessed doubts about the worth of personal involvement in the Vietnam War. But the propaganda and drugs he fed on did not create a freer man but one enslaved to new ideals. The prevailing attitude was, "If being a man meant going off to war to kill, he wanted nothing to do with it." Not surprising! At this time many seriously questioned adulthood. Some still haven't grown up. It was a confusing time for many. For some it still is.

Men, especially older white men, generally have a bad reputation in our culture. The warrior image according to "new age" authorities is the cause for all wars. Women, they say, have never been the cause of a war. The socially re-engineered "soft" man that the women's lib movement promoted has been bought into by many men. So why is there still such a lack of peace in our culture as compared with the previous 50 years? As the feminists approach age 50 they seem to be even more unhappy.

Modern women have solidly convinced most of those who control our democracy that "soft" men make ideal mates. So why is divorce on the increase? Modern man in trying to please and attract the opposite sex has tried his best to conform to the wishes of women. "Liberated" women demand equality with men. They have "trained" their males how to behave. Most men really do want to please the women they love. We are more easily influenced than most women today seem to know. Yet training promoting fair play and equality is so often based on a fear of hearing what we truly believe deep within ourselves. An increasing number of men are on a path of self-destruction as we have let go of traditional values that worked for us in the past. War threatens us all, especially women with their greater value placed on security. It is noteworthy that as society has accepted this new man concept, the effects have been negative: murder, rape, high-school dropout and crime rates are rising.

"Soft" man looks good on the outside. He sounds gentle, tender, caring and sensitive to the emotional needs of women. He says he doesn't want to pollute or fight in wars. He can fake an attitude of peace.

However, there is a hitch to all this hype. Modern man has not become more free. He seems more enslaved, definitely less happy. These new ideas give a false impression of who he is called to be. Man is naturally a warrior, a trapper with a flare for "the hunt." He constantly fights an inherent impulse to strike out on an adventure which intuitively he knows will lead him closer to his real self — perhaps even his God. Every man despite his outside protest knows inwardly there is a God. He dreams of living independently of society's handouts. He hates the thought of being a ward of the state. Only as he moves closer to the God society seems to say doesn't really exist, can he begin to experience reality. He then finds that he really can depend upon Him for everything for which "the system" wants him to depend on it.

Society is afraid of true "manliness." We live in a paranoid world that fears the truly successful man because he can't be controlled. Society has a right to be afraid because we are dealing with many males who have not surrendered to God's will for their lives. But instead of crying out to their Creator the world resorts to the unworkable solution of trying to change the basic makeup of man. This attempt to do a "makeover" of men is a form of rebellion against God because it ignores God's solution for man's problems. God does have the answer to this image problem. Yet prophesy is clear, society will continue to ignore His solution. Man will look for still newer ways to re-engineer millions of men to conform to its image of what the world needs in order to survive.

The warrior has become the scapegoat for most of man's ills. The liberal community believes strongly that this new concept of man must be accepted at all costs to preserve our species. Through this process of mass change modern man is being swept away from the purposes of what God intended for man's life on planet Earth.

THE MODEL WARRIOR

So what is a "warrior" really supposed to be like? He can't be a man bent on polluting, fighting, killing, and abusing. Conservatives agree here with liberals. What is the ideal man?

George Leonard, a World War II pilot, in an Esquire article, "The Warrior" (July 1986) wrote about a group of

Army Green Berets. The following is their definition of the ideal warrior. They came up with this definition:

> Our ideal warrior has loyalty, patience, intensity, calmness, compassion and will. A true warrior knows himself and his limitations. Self-mastery should be a warrior's central motivation. He is always practicing, always seeking to hone his skills, so as to become the best possible instrument for accomplishing his mission. The warrior takes calculated risks, and tests himself repeatedly. He believes in something greater than himself: a religion, a cause. He does not worship violence, but he is at home with it. He may snivel or complain, but he is not a victim.

These men from an elite branch of military service came close to the mark with this definition. We need, however, to add a spiritual dimension.

THE TOUCH OF A MAN

Of the many differences between men and women one is worth mentioning now. Men are usually more "soulish," on the other hand women rely more often on their feelings and intuition. A woman's ability to operate wisely from intuition often confounds a man. More often than not, we men need to lay hands on something in a tangible way before believing in it. This difference prohibits many men from coming close to the "ideal warrior" goal. There are definite times when a man needs to rely on his intuitive instincts which will sharpen as danger approaches. Yet most are not trained in and have not practiced for this eventuality. To depend on your mind alone during these dangerous times invites a disasterous outcome. A classic example is evident in the old patriarch's writings in chapter 32 of the Book of Exodus.

When Moses didn't come back down from the mountain at the expected moment, his own brother and other leaders took matters into their own hands. Moses was up on the mountain getting instructions from God. He took too long as far as his followers were concerned. Either God didn't show, or they thought Moses was distroyed. Lacking patience they took matters into their own hands and began worshiping false idols.

These men couldn't physically touch God so they made false idols they could touch. An invisible God wasn't real enough for them. They collected everyone's golden earrings, throwing them into a pile. From this pile they melted and molded a representation for God in the form of a golden calf, though this directly contradicted His Commandments.

Today, modern man is doing it again. We are building worldly gods from our society's "golden earrings." These false idols come in many different forms and shapes. Yet they point solidly towards what we really value. They contain all the elements that drive men to be jealous of each other. Man's modern "earrings" dangle in front of our eyes tempting and dividing us. Class warfare is growing in our once more unified nation. These earthly gods cause more and more of us to center on self-realization, self-improvement, self discovery, in other words, self. Such human practices demonstrate that human nature remains unchanged from Moses' time. A man who knows nothing of God will ultimately center his life on self. He will imagine he can through driving ambition satisfy his desires in fierce competition with other men. Worldly men take pride in their wealth and abilities as compared to their competitors. They plot to seize their share of the man-made goods (gods) in existance. They cut themselves off from other men by building barriers of contrast. This is the new "warrior" that has emerged in today's Western civilization. There is a popular bumper sticker epitomizing this battle: "The one who dies with the most toys, wins!"

This built-in warrior spirit in all males is a call to adventure, the occasional fight, and sometimes all out war. If men can't have traditional kinds of war they will manufacture new ones, seemingly more civil to the naked eye but just as brutal to the spirit of men. This new form of competition has not turned out to be all that civil.

WAR!

Men crave passion! Passion that undresses every beautiful woman in sight is not what I am referring to. But a passion that challenges and pushes a man to begin a sincere search for the very best qualities lying deep within his spirit is the real thing. It can not be surpressed. We need to be encouraged to dive into healthy projects that unlease our raw emotions and interests. This will lead men to discover their true natures.

One male passion that societies of all ages have never been able to quiet is the insatiable desire for the "hunt," the need to conquer. This is why war has been a consistent activity over the centuries.

This is a major frustration for peace activists. They fervently desire to change man's viewpoint on war. Finding an alternative to man's need to bash and batter others into submission, is a consuming goal.

Men deprived of war will engineer other troubles to satisfy this inner urge. Unfortunately, many men construct conflicts within their own homes and families which are destructive to the wider culture. This certainly isn't God's image of what He desires for man. What then is needed?

This natural passion in men must be redirected into channels that help not hurt. They need to discover and live according to the precepts of the "ideal warrior." This comes about when men have a vision of what true manhood is. Traditional words such as loyalty, patience, passion, calmness, tenderness, compassion, will, and courage hint at the true direction of mature manhood.

MAN'S GREATEST FEAR

Men are designed by God to be "givers" rather than receivers. This is demonstrated by our biological makeup. Men have the "plumbing" to give; women, to receive. Men forced into the role of receivers find that role to be out of character and unnatural!

Healthy men instinctively fear becoming too reliant on women, or her substitute, the welfare system. The possibility of becoming too dependent physically, emotionally or spiritually is an uncomfortable proposition for the vibrant man. Such a dependent status would put him back under the care of a mother type. Men spent their youth reaching the point where they risk cutting loose from mom's "apron strings," the final proof of adulthood. Going backwards in this natural process causes a loss of internal respect for a man.

COURAGE

Courage is a virtue men talk about and want to display where given a fair chance to do so. Personally my favorite man of courage is Jesus Christ. All men have a basic need to display the level of courage He demonstrated. A major problem is the garbage that comes out of Hollywood concerning role models. Unhealthy views of reality are dealt with, because fiction sells. Typically, we see a man charging machine gun nests with bare hands and a bayonet clenched between his teeth. Falsifying the concept of courage is just one of the ways Hollywood fictionalizes the truth to our detriment.

Courage too often is misconstrued as a warlike quality unnecessary in times of relative peace and security. Courage, however, really has little to do with killing people and destroying property. Courage in its purest form is demonstrated by the man who stands by his convictions no matter the persecution or ridicule. The real hero acts as he believes he should, and not as others want him to behave in all circumstances. Jesus never killed anyone. But the courage He displayed is legendary. By going uncomplainingly to the cross to give His life for those unworthy of such love, He not only defined love but also true manhood in the process. There is no higher act of bravery and honor than His unselfish act of bravery. He laid aside the awesome power of God to show the reality of His Father's undying love for even the worst of us.

Corporal Bill Morgan, one of my squad leaders in Vietnam, displayed such unconditional courage. His love for several wounded Marines caught in a crossfire resulted in his death in 1969. His was clearly a sacrificial act. His diversionary tactic allowed wounded squad members to be pulled to safety off a "hot" jungle trail in S.E. Asia. In death he is greatly honored. Morgan received our nation's highest award for valor, the Congressional Medal of Honor. Courage is best explained by what one gives up, not by what one obtains.

Corporal Morgan, like Jesus Christ, gave his all. He stood unwavering in his conviction. What he believed in, he ultimately died for. His friends would go on living because of his unselfishness. He demonstrated true courage and manhood. He stands as a giant in my hall of heroes. The majority of the men I was privileged to command in combat were heroic when necessary. They may not have been placed by divine providence into a situation where they were able to excel and earn a decoration, but all but a few went through the daily drudgery in an uncomplaining manner. They were available when needed. How we handle drudgery shows the depth of our character. We have an inherited nature (2 Peter 1:5) and it is up to us to discipline ourselves with a gung-ho attitude to form good habits through diligence and concentration. If you can't do it alone as a civilian then join a tough organization like the Marines where supervision will develop diligent and positive character habits. Don't avoid tough challenges when your conscience says you need to be challenged, or the Lord may have to put you through the school called "hard knocks" to create the character He demands in His disciples.

Heroic humility is the great mark of a true man. Neither brawn nor brain can accomplish great feats. They are a matter of "heart."

Thomas Merton summed up the courage I speak of in his book, *The Seeds of Contemplation*. He said, "A man cannot enter into the deepest center of himself and pass through that center into God, unless he is able to pass entirely out of himself and give himself to other people in the purity of selfless love."

Next we need to look at the true source of legitimate male bonding. Bonding is one of the great keys to why the Marines are able to prevail in combat and for over 220 years have been in the forefront of America's war efforts.

A BAND OF BROTHERS

"So then you are no longer strangers and aliens, but you are fellow citizens, with the saints, and are of God's household."
Ephesians 2:9

Have you heard the term, "blood brother?" Groups of men over the ages have used this type of bonding to seal lifelong commitments by their members. By sacrificially cutting the flesh and intermingling their blood, they become brothers (bonded) in a very special way. In this chapter we will view what is natural in forming strong male relations beyond the traditional family before dealing in the last chapter with what is unnatural.

Two famous Christian missionaries to Africa, Stanley and Livingston, stood in the midst of many native tribal societies to cut themselves ceremonially, blending their blood with tribal chiefs for the opportunity to bring the Gospel of Christ into their territories. In return they received protection and blessings for life in their target territories! By relating to the tribal chiefs in this fashion many missionary opportunities were opened up for them and others who followed.

The unselfish act of showing unity by entering a blood covenant enabled them to travel freely throughout tribal territories without fear of attack. Both men became honored guests of each tribal chief they bonded with, in fact, blood family members. A tribal chief who bonded through blood became duty bound to defend his new blood brother in his tribe's territory for life under penalty of death from his family if he failed to do so. The blood family's honor was that important. As strange as it may seem to outsiders, the military boot camp experience has the effect of uniting recruits going through in the same way. The saying "Once a Marine always a Marine" shows the awesome unifying power of that experience.

A "blood-bought" friendship can never be dismissed and it will never die. In 1978, though I had been a practicing Christian all my conscious life in a religious sense, the death of Jesus Christ on the cross became a personal reality to me emotionally for the first time as an adult. I realized in a new way that Jesus, by His unselfish act of allowing His pure and innocent blood to be spilled on a cross, died and took upon Himself the penalties that I was otherwise faced with. He died in my place! An innocent man, dying for the guilty! His awesome sacrifice for me filled me with a deep brotherly love for Him. For the first time in a deep new way I realized that "Greater love has no one than this, that one lay down his life for his brothers (John 15:13)."

I really knew for the first time that Jesus was "duty bound" to defend me after I had entered into a blood covenant with Him. Just like those tribal chiefs defended Stanley and Livingston because he had entered into a covenant with them. I had accepted the truth that He died as my "stand-in." Jesus and I are blood brothers! I slowly came to realize I had also entered a wonderful blood-bought brotherhood with other Christian believers across religious boundaries who had also seen and also accepted this life-changing truth. Sadly, I also recognized many didn't know this deep truth that I loved dearly.

THE POWER OF BLOOD

When two people understand the power of the blood which Jesus Christ shed for each person on earth, it makes all the difference in the quality of their relationships. In a way, this relationship-building method is exactly why many American street gang members cut their wrists and allow their blood to flow together. They are trying to promote a form of unity and devotion to become more of a family. They know the power of spilled blood and a solemn oath to effect such a change. As street gangs who are bonded through violence, there is bonding that takes place between persons based on a sexual relationship that is outside the God-ordained marriage covenant. This bonds their souls to each other, and puts people in harm's way. The street gang members and others who bond in other unholy ways are placed outside the protection provided by obedience to God's Ten Commandments.

The level of brotherhood fostered within the U.S. Marine Corps is achieved a positive way. The Corps doesn't encourage the actual cutting of flesh, but disciplines the flesh in other ways. Through it's world-famous boot camp experience, bonding is achieved. The toughness of this experience is one reason why the Marine Corps is so highly effective in breaking down divisive barriers such as race among most individuals.

I have seen men risk death for brothers with a different skin color under fire in combat. Men who face death (enemy fire) for general reasons like country, the U.S. Constitution, family back home, duty, honor, or brotherhood, seldom will have the confidence under fire of a brother who has the kind of love for another that caused Christ to lay down His life for us.

Men in the armed forces who may not know the truth about Christ may still be required to risk death to keep an earthly agreement with another. How much more a brother who does know Christ as his personal savior should be willing to risk his life for proper spiritual commitments like the marriage covenant and legitimate oaths such as the military enlistment contract! The power of unity that the blood bond of Christ gives to brothers who come into the full light of Christ is wonderfully different ("see how they love one another"). If you don't feel this way about born again Christians I question whether you have been born again. This brotherhood is quite real and exists in the present day Corps as well as beyond. America is better off with such a brotherhood in its midst. And, it is a brotherhood any man can join.

In times of trouble a good family draws closer together. The blood covenant relationship creates that important family bond each of us needs away from home to cope with the real difficulties of life in a combat zone. Where a true brotherhood exists nothing is more valued than the safety, trust and security each member has through his spiritual family ties. When trouble looms such a man knows he will be rescued, if not by a human brother-in-arms, than certainly by God, the head of the family. God's wonderful promise to come to the aid of His sons and daughters is a reality among such a band of brothers ... it is expected and humbly appreciated by all who really believe. One of my favorite Psalms in reference to this is Psalm 50:14-15, "Offer to God praise as your sacrifice and fulfill your vows to the Most High. Then call upon me in time of distress; I will rescue you, and you shall glorify me."

When a man for the first time really sees this truth, he becomes a blood brother to Jesus Christ in a special new way. He joins a band of men and women who have experienced this new birth. Unfortunately, there is too often a vast difference between the ritual ceremony of baptism/confirmation within a church body and the heart knowledge that allows the recipient to experience this new birth personally. It's that critical 18 inches from the head to the heart. When you actually experience this new birth you truly do see life through new eyes. Your world becomes very different than it was previously.

I am honored to be a United States Marine. But, I commend to all who have not yet entered the spiritual brotherhood of which I speak, a personal search effort until this new birth is truly discovered. There is no higher honor in this life than to be an adopted son of God through entry into the blood covenant relationship with Christ.

MEN OF MERCY

In the last chapter I will address sexual bonding experiences that separate males who taste its "forbidden fruit." Males unwilling to be freed from such bondage are a threat to proper bonding experiences between men necessary for significant strides in the progress of society. There is a principle which is fundamental for success in challenging men toward progress in overcoming personal and organizational faults in wholesome ways. Leaders who fully grasp and implement this principle make more progress in inspiring others than those who fail to grasp the significance of this principle.

Men band together as brothers in a shared faith to accomplish all kinds of purposes. But if their leaders do not understand and impliment this very crucial principle their organizational purpose will always fall short of its potential. The principle is mercy.

Concerning unsanctioned practices men must be encouraged to be merciful towards the shortcoming of other men while judging and attempting to correct their non-productive behavior. Balancing mercy with judgment is hard to do. The tendency is to err on the side of mercy which the reprobates will take advantage of every time. Such a tendency in leadership will ruin the esprit de corps of a unit even more quickly than erring on the side of judgment.

There are those whose strong ego refuses to admit to any wrongdoing. Men who don't show mercy are very difficult to work with. Mercy is crucial to the mental health of those called upon to execute life or death decisions. Short of unwavering mercy nothing sane gets resolved in combat.

In the absence of a genuine brotherhood few have sufficient strength to handle effectively the really tough emotional issues that can surface. Unlawful killing, i.e. murder, is too often perpetrated by men within brotherhoods with what they perceive as lofty goals. Murder never is justified by the result. It is always an abomination to God.

Mercy is the quality of showing genuine care and kindness toward those who don't deserve it. With that definition in mind how would you deal with a peer who disappointed you in a major way through behavior you find personally abhorrent?

Only where an adequate level of mercy is displayed by a leader is it possible for subordinates to lay aside the natural bitterness and resentment that wrongdoing provokes in those hurt by the wrongdoers. Wrongdoers who wish to change and be reconciled with those they have let down will become hardened and grow worse where they are not forgiven. Selfishness is natural and where not properly countered will grow into arrogant pride which is hated by God and will make it difficult to establish the unity necessary for organizational effectiveness. Leaders especially are clearly instructed by their consciences to bring a spirit of mercy into the decision-making process. Unit survival often depends on mercy, which is often in short supply in the combat environment.

God wants every human on earth saved. But the Bible clearly shows hardened sinners on a broad path bound towards Hell. How on earth can such be saved when those with the inclination to set a right example isolate themselves from wrongdoers through a lack of mercy? The Apostle Paul sent this word to the Corinthians, "I have written you in my letter not to associate with sexually immoral people—not at all meaning the people of this world who are immoral, or the greedy and swindlers, or idolaters. In that case you would have to leave this world. But now I am writing you that you must not associate with anyone who calls himself a brother but is sexually immoral or greedy, an idolater or a slanderer, a drunkard or a swindler. With such a man do not even eat. What business is it of mine to judge those outside the church? Are you not to judge those inside? God will judge those outside (I Cor. 5:9-13 NIV)."

HIGHER PURPOSE
FOR BAND OF BROTHERS

Many fraternal brotherhoods perform a social function. Many like the Marines have a higher purpose such as the defense of a nation. A mature "band of brothers" can demonstrate a level of mercy during the execution of terrible judgment.

The Christian's primary "role model" must be Jesus even while honoring organizational leaders whose prime example is not Christ. Jesus came 20 centuries ago not only to form the Church, but also to provide His disciples with current, timely examples of how to live responsibly in every age. Today's calendar goes backwards and forwards from that point in history where He entered time for that remarkable 33-year period. History is His story.

Christ demonstrated awesome mercy and still managed to accomplish exactly what he was sent by His Father to do. Satan's considerable skills were massed against Him to prevent Him from doing what was necessary to pay for our salvation. But He accomplished it anyway. God come in human flesh could have inflicted terrible harm on those who opposed Him. Instead he laid down His terrible two-edged sword at that time to demonstrate the awesome power of mercy to effect change. Wrongdoers who ignore this lesson, make an awful mistake if they choose to forget that He has promised to return and wield that sword of judgment. We are not excused from demonstrating mercy in our responsible actions as we under legal authority execute judgment against improper actions on the field of combat.

THE POWER OF LIFE AND DEATH

Men in combat take on the responsibility of judges with the power of life and death. Soldiers need the same level of discrimination as judges. Too often war zones are occupied by the young and innocent. Loaded weapons in the hands of the irresponsible can cause great havoc. Soldiers seldom have the authority to shoot at everything that moves. Target selection is almost always a high priority for leaders.

Men in combat who profess to practice the Christian faith are held to a higher standard by even non-Christians who know of the mercy of Jesus Christ. Yet too often so-called Christians bloody the name above all names by careless, mean-spirited abuse of power. A fellow unit member who is obviously out of order must be challenged using the organization's standard operating procedure. Inappropriate behavior in others, especially in combat, can not be tolerated. Such times present opportunities for Christian witness not available in more peaceful settings. Even then the offender must not be the target. The inappropriate behavior is what should be zeroed in on. At these times you will be effective only if you have previously sharpened your level of compassion through practice in less crucial settings.

Love the sinner, hate the sin. This is a principle of life easily lost sight of in civilian life through compromise. But it is crucial in combat where every man is essential, though not all are at the front lines.

Marines must uphold the well-known physical, intellectual, and moral standards of the United States Marine Corps especially during difficult times!

The only real hope for males ambushed by growing levels of perversion in society is a revelation of the truth. Men locked into abnormal bondages are headed toward death and seem not to know it. Their perverse practices create intense internal conflict and doublemindedness. Reprobates can only deal with such perversion through denial. This denial creates pain in others concerned for their welfare. All inherently know that such behavior will eventually be severely judged by God.

No therapy, procedure, "cure" or compromise within our human health care system will fully redeem those caught up in unsavory lifestyles (death styles). There will be a great need to take care of the health care needs of those who refuse to live clean lives. But there is a far greater need for healing of souls and spirits before their appointed meeting with death. At that time it is too late to change one's ways. No matter one's current station in life those in darkness will increasingly encounter unhealthiness. Abnormal sexual appetites cause compromise that eventually spins one out of control.

TRUTH IS THE SAFE COURSE

All are challenged by society's spirit of compromise. So, truth is the only safe course. Don't sympathize with one caught up in perversion of any kind. Bondage is evil in any form. Empathy is a requirement of successful leadership. No real change ever takes place until one looks beyond the human system for answers. Those who are hurting badly and searching for answers will come to those with strong levels of mercy. Those in the grip of unhealthy appetites are pathetic. They desperately need Christ. Only in His arms will they begin to experience real relief from their misery.

Many Christians have had bad initial experiences with rejection from attempts to share lifegiving truth. They pass up later opportunities to witness because of mistakes in judgment at the beginning. Fear of rejection only helps the destroyer. It is up to God to change aberrant behavior. But God does need the courageous to cooperate under His anointing in doing the work of God. Frontline enemy troops are aggressive in their desire to convert you to "their truth." You must take advantage of opportunities God provides to show them His truth.

The Marine Corps promotion policy is up or out. Christ's ultimate standard, unlike the human standard of the Marine Corps, can't be compromised by any political system. It doesn't matter how much compromise you think you see in evidence. God Himself is not doing any compromising of His standards. Take comfort in this fact. The coming failures in America's political and religious systems are not a problem to God. His ability to accomplish His desires will only increase under pressure. God shows mercy for a season toward all His creatures. In the same way He expects you to be merciful while remaining uncompromising concerning the truth. Leave judgment in His hands. "Vengeance is mine, I will repay, saith the Lord (Romans 12:19 KJV)." The Bible shows clearly that He does get around to judgment even where we are sure He is often far too slow.

In the present political atmosphere, unity will not be achieved or maintained through political compromise in or outside our military system. No amount of dutiful adherence to obvious compromise will overcome civilian mistakes in managing the military system. Justice is not likely to be restored to its former level where compromised from outside the military system due to civilian errors in judgment. Those within the system must show a strong commitment during the difficult and immoral times ahead.

DIVISIVE AND EXPLOSIVE ISSUES GROWING

The divisive and explosive issues that separate us are growing. Recorded prophesy in Scripture will not go away. Domestic enemy advocates lead the charge for an ever increasing share of our finite health care system. At the same time they demonstrate a growing unwillingness to live healthy life styles. When the majority forfeits their right to say enough is enough, the cost of health care will at some point break the bank. This is a problem for the ten percent who live as if there is no tomorrow, refusing the clear warnings of health care experts (i.e. smoking, excessive drinking, drug use, illicit sex, etc.). It is not reasonable that we who live in moderation should pay for their excesses. Those who lust for what is unhealthy will eventually experience major illness. So it is kindness toward them to hate the effect their perverted appetites have on them and others under their control.

The lessons of history clearly show hard times ahead for those living beyond the edge. The present political system for the most part refuses to treat a growing number of health care concerns as the epidemics they have become, so the system will break down. This will force believers to lean more heavily on Jesus for protection.

There is a real enemy loose in our country. Hollywood knows his name, Satan. He commands far more attention than does Christ in their films. He must get perverse pleasure when he sees moral leaders abandoning their assigned territory in protest of society's ever lowering standards. Can anyone but God really lower earth's standards? What is the consequence for the one who throws in the towel in protest? It only furthers the enemy's cause. Possess the courage to live your moral convictions at what ever level of command you find yourself. You can make a difference even when you think you aren't. Make Satan's mission more difficult by standing firm. When moral men leave military service, standards are lowered because those less informed become more vulnerable to the influence of evil through the decreased level of good example. Good example is paramount. Those with base appetites must not be allowed to dominate a critical field of influence like the military. Increasing levels of immorality in the military will eventually have a terrible effect on the civilian society that turns from Christ.

Increasingly the power elite seems to view the American military as a mercenary force to be used anywhere they decide. Do you want American sons and daughters to become part of another French Foreign Legion? That is happening because our military power is increasingly falling into the hands of men whose life demonstrates a willingness to compromise with evil. What Psalm 12:8 talks about could become an increasing nightmare. It says, "The wicked freely strut about when what is vile is honored among men."

HATING COMPROMISE

God really does use and will continue to call men of integrity into military service no matter how bad immorality and open hostility toward Christ grows because of Satan's infiltration. A moral man, like Michael New who refused to wear a UN patch because it violated his oath of enlistment, feels a natural rage when he sees evil triumph politically. When civilian leaders compromise by lowering standards where is it safe to hide? This cannot be the reason for leaving one's calling if it is to military service. I hate compromise. Michael New refused to compromise. I would love to see our military remain in the hands of men of integrity who refuse to compromise with any form of evil.

The civilian church in America has a good understanding of the importance of chaplains in helping to ensure a proper moral climate in our armed forces for young men and women. It is frustrating to see military leadership increasingly tied up morally through political compromise. A relationship with the military is important in helping the civilian church become more militant in promoting its core values in the larger society.

Overcoming fear is a very logical next step after achieving unity. Only then can we come against "sin in the camp."

FEAR NO EVIL

**"God has not given us a spirit of fear; but
of power, and of love, and a sound mind."
2 Timothy 1:7**

In combat the proportion of fear a trained man experiences is in relation to his nearness to the enemy. Obviously, exposure to imminent death or injury will create the most fear. It's obvious that the civilian and combat environments are different in their capacity to create fear. Few would dispute this fact. Because men entering the army come from civilian backgrounds they obviously need special training in preparation to handle the potential of massive, enduring fear that combat environment provides. Even after discharge from military service the effectiveness of such training remains. This is continually shown by the high percentage of former servicemen who respond out of a civilian crowd of bystanders during a civil emergency. Former servicemen are also found in high risk occupations like police work in numbers way out of proportion to their percentage of the larger population. They have learned how to cope with and overcome fear. They are good at it.

Fear is every man's enemy whether civilian or soldier. The final fear we all face is death. We all eventually die. Fearful people can and do infect others with their anxieties, tensions and unbeliefs even in the relative safety of civilian life. Believers and unbelievers can be grouped into one of two categories: There are those who can turn most occasions into a cause for worry. There are others who according to the worriers are not bright enough to be worried. The tension between these two differing groups is obvious as they go about their daily routines. The combat term for the worrier who becomes terrorized by danger to the point of paralysis is **coward**.

Fear spreads like wildfire when courage is silenced in dangerous moments. The courageous must speak out at such moments in history or things take a turn for the worse for everyone. Good, but timid, men die needlessly as a result of unchecked fear. This is as true in the civilian world as in combat zones. Your fear can cause another to fail when he should have succeeded.

How men deal with their fears ultimately determines the outcome of most human endeavors. Therefore, fear is a subject worthy of close inspection by leaders desiring to expand their knowledge of vital character attributes such as boldness and courage. This is true whether or not a leader ever expects to experience terror equivalent to the fright one contends with during a fire fight.

The apocalyptic end-time prophecies in the Bible have captured the interest if not respect of thinking men. There was an ancient doctor by the name of Luke who wrote several books, later canonized as part of the New Testament. In his book entitled, The Gospel of St. Luke, Jesus spoke about future events to occur in history. I find it interesting that the Lord made specific reference to the level of fear that would occur in some men near the end of human history. We may be closer to that time than most in this generation realize. "There will be signs in the sun, moon and the stars. On the earth, nations will be in anguish, distraught at the roaring of the sea and the waves. Men will die of fright in anticipation of what is coming upon the earth. ...When these things begin to happen, stand erect and hold your heads high, for your deliverance is near at hand (Luke 21:25,26,28)."

HOW TO HANDLE FEAR

The Bible frequently addresses the subject of fear. In the above quote it says that when others are paralyzed by fear on the terrible "Day of Judgment" we can stand erect and hold our heads high for we will know that our deliverance is at hand.

Just how do we muster up this kind of courage when by all natural logic we should be so paralyzed by fear we cannot move? By practicing bravery during times of relative peace a believer will experience the "deliverance" in minor ways talked about in Scripture. From these small beginnings he will learn and will be able to hold his head up bravely in spite of all that could ever come against him in more difficult times. It is important for us to know how to handle fear. Let's focus now more closely on the anatomy of this culprit called **fear**.

If there are men who can display such courage in the fearful circumstances ahead, a worthy military commander should want to recruit such courageous men. A smart leader will want his share of such men to ensure an adequate esprit de corps (spirit of unity) within his own unit. Imagine a military force made up of men with hearts so brave and strong? The honor, trust, and respect rendered such men in a unit would be supernatural to behold, a comfort and great blessing to those less brave in times of great danger.

Marine Corps training teaches its members offensive and defensive survival tactics, how to fire and maneuver, proper action to take in ambushes, how to "dig in" for protection from enemy fire, to name a few of the combat skills addressed. None of these abilities cause one to be without fear when experiencing a terrifying combat circumstance. Ask any Marine if he was afraid when enemy mortar fire came down upon his fortified position. A normal man would say, "yes!" No matter how much physical protection, experience, and training one has, any man in his right mind will have normal fear about his safety in the midst of such an enemy firestorm. It's natural to experience fear in certain situations. So we're obviously looking for another kind of courage, or absence of fear mentioned in the Bible verses above.

ANATOMY OF FEAR

A moderate sense of fear is considered normal, even healthy. It may be an emotion or an awareness of impending danger. It's a defense mechanism. It may be characterized by the pounding heart, flushed face, and sweaty palms in anticipation of being called on in class or asked to make a speech in front of a group of people. Or, it could be the soul-screaming terror that can change your life forever and leave a trail of haunting memories in each of your future steps. Men who have survived close-in combat have no problems identifying that kind of fear.

Fears can be acute or chronic, and a reaction to real or imagined circumstances. The control of fear in our lives depends largely on how well fear is managed within the environment in which we find ourselves.

ANATOMY OF COURAGE

To better understand fear it is best to define courage. Courage can be defined as "the inner conviction to stand up for the truth, regardless of the consequences." When a man stands up for his convictions he will naturally feel anxieties, and fear the repercussions of his stand from those who oppose his point of view. One's spiritual commitment to honesty and truth must overshadow the natural emotions that flow with the rejection of the less committed. The man of courage presses on knowing he will have opposition from those with different underlying assumptions about the meaning of life, even his own family.

If a man operates solely on his natural instincts he will not overcome fear. He cannot because his reflexes and responses are bound to function in the natural ways of this earthly realm. Only by committing the natural reactions and what his body, memory and spirit have experienced in this physical life to the Spirit of God, can he overcome the power fear will have in his life. Only then can he begin to walk supernaturally and thereby begin to cope in a new, more powerful way. In the beginning doubt is normal, but will lessen. Ultimately it will disappear for the one who continues down the path of destiny. When a believer commits his fear reactions to God, he will begin to react in a supernatural way instead of "re-acting" mainly through natural restimulations such as the adrenalin rush.

FEAR AND FATIGUE

The military stresses physical fitness for a reason. First there is the scheduled physical training. Athletes preparing for a contest and soldiers preparing for combat are forced to a higher level of individual accountability. One becomes responsible for his time in a way that those not subject to such challenges rarely experience. One learns that adrenalin rushes may temporarily quiet the queasy stomach, but provide no long-term peace of mind. Fear and fatigue often come at you hand in hand during such stressful times. The soldier in poor physical condition is more susceptible to fear. By itself fear will cause fatigue. Together these two can incapacitate the poorly conditioned person physically, emotionally, and spiritually. A man will set himself up to be victimized at a later date if he shows a lack of discipline during less challenging periods. Those who cooperate in getting into the best physical and spiritual shape possible prior to entry into combat lessen their susceptibility to the spirit of fear and its twin companion, fatigue.

So what about the souls of men? Not the spirit of man, but the soul. We'll define the soul as one's mind, will, and emotions. This aspect of man's being is as critical, or more, than his physical conditioning. The soul needs to be disciplined daily. Otherwise it gets out of whack and begins to drag down the spirit! The Marine Corps spends as much time conditioning the soul through training as a man's body. But one critical aspect of this conditioning process is left totally in the care of each individual. That is his spiritual knowledge. Yes, at the battalion and squadron level there is an assigned chaplain. But most everything he does, although of utmost importance, is voluntarily attended.

One who lacks spiritual knowledge is in bad shape, yet may have no conscious clue! Don't neglect your self-training in this area. You need to continually expand your level of spiritual knowledge. A vigorous pursuit of the virtue called wisdom leads to an increase in one's understanding of the truth. Wisdom will come to the one who chooses to walk this path. A wise person conditions his (or her) soul to stand tall against the debilitating effects of fear, and other manifestations of spiritual weakness. David, in the Old Testament Psalms gives evidence that he knew the soul needed to be brought under daily discipline. He wrote, "Bless the Lord, O my soul...(Psalm 103:1)."

Once again, to illustrate the value of spiritual exercise, I quote a spiritual champion of the first century, the Apostle Paul, "For physical training is of some value, but godliness has value for all things, holding promise for both the present life and the life to come (1 Timothy 4:8 NIV)."

THE BENEFITS OF STRONG LEADERSHIP

In the presence of strong, physical leadership there will be a general absence of fear and fatigue. This is even more true with strong spiritual leadership. There are those pastors who provide mostly a diet of milk to their adult flock. Other pastors provide a solid diet of meat and potatoes. Discernment is needed in selecting your pastor. What level of spiritual maturity do you seek in the denomination (body of believers) you have selected? Pastors are spiritual athletic coaches. Some can only prepare you for kindergarten. Others can prepare you for the Olympics. Pastors according to the book of Malachi will be held accountable before God for how they helped you in preparing your soul and spirit for the good race of life. Will you be able to cross the finish line?

I must warn you. A pastor who approaches this high calling as a mere job will do you little good for those emergencies we all must face (1 Cor 10:13). Fear and fatigue will bounce with sudden swiftness during such times of danger. It takes strong moral and spiritual leaders to prepare you for such times.

Your chances of survival and prosperity in times of real combat depend on the quality of your leadership training. Where the church is viewed as weak it needs an infusion of militancy. Where an army is viewed as weak and corrupt it needs an infusion of morality. A strong church and a strong armed force are critical for health and survival in America. When great danger comes it is too late to think about getting these two vital institutions back in shape. That is why through history democracies have never lasted more than two hundred years. The church and the military, two most critical arms of our society, must begin to respect each other's abilities and contributions more then is presently the case. We stay divided at our peril.

HOW WILLING ARE YOU TO BE STRETCHED?

As I look back over my military experience from a perspective of more than 30 years I see three military-style baptisms experienced by those who make it into the pages of history. This is true whether at the local or international level. The two men of destiny I have highlighted in this book experienced all three of these physical baptismal experiences. General John Lejeune and Lt. Colonel Pete Ellis, like all service members experienced the initial screening baptism of "boot camp" or "officer candidate training." Most members of the armed forces experience only this first baptismal initiation, serve in an acceptable manner their period of enlistment and then are discharged honorably. They may never have to experience combat and may not have benefitted by the increased maturity that comes from private mentoring from an experienced senior up the line.

The second military baptism is when a man is taken under the wing of one with more experience. An experienced veteran who is attracted to a junior out of admiration and who takes time to work with a novice above and beyond the general training offered to all men is receiving and giving something special. Why would a senior do such a thing?

Such an extra effort to help a junior is rare. It will only come about when an experienced senior finds the personality of a junior especially attractive. Such a bond can be like that received by a favored son. Where the mentoring comes from a genuine and mutual respect for each other the junior has in my experience usually separated himself from his peers in a very special way by demonstrating a spirit of service or volunteerism far above that displayed by the norm. It may be deserved or undeserved. But either way is a blessing from God. Finally a man's character can be further shaped by the baptism of fire we call "combat." This is the severest testing of character known to mankind apart from martyrdom. Many more seem to fail this test then pass it. In combat a loss has greater impact then with sporting contests.

Direct experience is good. But it is even better to learn a valuable lesson through the experience of another. Good books offer a wealth of valuable personal experience. That is why the Marine Corps has a mandatory reading list as a part of their promotional system. What father doesn't encourage a son he is pleased with to seek wisdom by studying the ancient texts himself? The text of highest regard in the life of wise men I have been drawn to has been the sacred Scriptures, the Bible. Many, however are careful about sharing this truth. Why "cast your pearls before swine" they feel. A man can go through his entire life admiring a man from a distance and never learn that his strength is drawn from daily time in the Bible. In that collection of ancient books you will discover that the man found pleasing to God is not necessarily the one found pleasing to men. Every day the world's leaders pass by men who are pleasing to the common man yet are being overlooked by their superiors. Why? They may not know how to or desire not to play the political game. The Holy Spirit is a mentor to whom we all have access, though few go to Him. Jesus commanded us not to represent His Father (Acts 1:4-5) until we received a new, special relationship with Him through power on high.

One of the Bible's clearest messages is that the "Fear of the Lord [respect for God] is the beginning of all wisdom (Psalm 111:10)." Could wisdom be an Old Testament name for the Holy Spirit? (Reflect on Proverbs, chapter eight.)

This special gift, the fear of the Lord, is the primary lesson I learned from my father. Yet it wasn't "verbally" taught by him. It was the consistency of his Sunday routine and a certain difference in his manner over time that I picked up on. My extensive analysis of our two men of destiny shows both were used mightily by God. However, one was blessed with longevity of life, the other man was not. Even more fearful is the fact that I have assurance of only one man's eternal destiny. I have never met a man that I wish to experience the eternal fires of hell. Only one of God's Ten Commandments has a blessing of longevity attached to it. It may or may not explain the difference between the different rewards received by Lejeune and Ellis in life. There are many scriptural keys that may hint at the difference in the two men's earthly rewards, but we'll not know the entire story in this life for sure. God's word says, "Honor your father and mother all the days of your life and you will receive longevity and happiness...(Deuteronomy 5:16)." This could explain the difference in their longevity.

Two additional verses from God's Word could provide clues to their difference in longevity. Our two heroes obviously had great respect for each other as does the entire Marine Corps who know of their individual accomplishments. They accomplished a great deal together because of their mutual respect for each other despite a quite different moral outlook. Respect is a strong indicator of true love. Because this book is about staying alive in combat while doing your duty I must address the obvious fact that men have different outlooks towards eternity which obviously affects personal longevity.

"The Lord loves those that hate evil; he guards the lives of his faithful ones; from the hand of the wicked He delivers them (Psalm 97:10)."

"Because he loves me," says the Lord, "I will rescue him; I will protect him, for he acknowledges my name (Psalm 91:14 NIV)."

THE PATH OF DESTINY

We are all called to a path of destiny. The right path requires courage no matter your present environment or station in life. Do you have the courage to really speak out, and live your moral convictions? There are no easy shortcuts in life. Over time, nature will slow down and finally stop evil by coming against those men who get ahead by ignoring the accepted norms and taking moral shortcuts.

God has an exciting plan for each man's future, no matter the present circumstance he finds himself in. God clearly is no respecter of persons. He will give you what he has promised and given to other heroes of the Word who paid the price. He is looking for obedient sons and daughters in this present age to receive their promised inheritance.

I am constantly amazed at the parallels between the natural and the supernatural world. Many Americans at least give lip service to the Christian sacrament of identification with Christ through baptism in water. Many received this baptism as infants. Our adult faith, however, may only be a shadow of that of a beloved parent or grandparent. Their faith somehow never became real to us. We may continue along in their outward religious routine. Or we may give up our parents' faith routine altogether as obsolete because of its lack of evident power in our own lives.

Well into adulthood I had no clear understanding of the importance of additional baptisms beyond what my denomination passed on to me with the best of intentions through their sacred ritual. My relationship with God hadn't become real though I thought it was. I knew that acknowledging God was important and continued to do so. My faith hadn't become personal in spite of my devotional efforts. In blind faith, I continued my childhood practice expecting someday my practice would lead to more. That "more" only arrived after I became desperate enough to dig it out in a whole new way. I began reading the Bible at the age of 37. When I moved beyond my traditional religious rut, God faithfully met me where I was spiritually. He is so faithful in His patience towards me. Should I be any less patient with those I am responsible for loving?

The Bible is clear about additional baptisms (Hebrews 6:1) for the one who digs it out. It's a personal thing. Don't wait for your pastor to enlighten you in a Sunday sermon. I was more than faithful to attend church, which I still do. I hope you don't have to wait as long as I did. Discovering the excitement of a genuine faith is wonderful.

More in the civilian and military church population need to get desperate in their seeking of God. Only then will our country be in stronger moral shape. More in the church must get serious about looking different from the unchurched world in the area of being a personal example of righteous living. Will we or will we not learn the example from the Old Testament that deception (spiritual blindness) is a death wish? Only a remnant of Israelites avoided destruction or captivity. Are we as a people making the very same mistakes? God's judgment on our nation is staring us in the face and so few seem to be aware of the danger we are in. The soldier who lacks the heart to discipline himself will never grow sufficiently strong and disciplined to distinguish himself above and beyond in combat duty if called to perform. Such a man is only lukewarm, a dangerous position to be in according to Christ, when the threat of danger becomes real. At that point additional preparation is too little and too late. From my personal observations, our country is getting sicker and sicker. We seem to have too many civilians in Christ and not enough soldiers in Christ. Will you seek additional baptisms to prepare you to operate not in the rear but out in front? More leaders are needed. Are you up to the challenge?

SOURCES OF PERSONAL POWER

There are three sources of power available for those who desire more personal power. We receive one type of power through formal study (the pursuit of education). I'll name this, **Knowledge Power**. The second source comes to the person who receives rank or title by appointment. It is **Position Power**. Such power influences the people in the sphere of influence assigned them. Position power enhances ability to use knowledge power. Peers and people under them must listen and respect their opinion.

But, if you are to have full power, there is a third source of power that becomes increasingly evident as you advance into middle age. I was growing aware I was without it in areas I desired to improve but couldn't. Gradually I became discouraged by attempts to capture that elusive successful attitude. In my attempt to advance up the pecking order or corporate chain of command of my chosen profession, I had never achieved lasting satisfaction at new levels. With each new success I did not find the lasting fulfillment that I had expected to be there.

Over time I met some others who had the power of personality I longed for but didn't feel I had in the measure I sought. My early impression was that it was a matter of time, education, and experience. But this was proving over and over not to be the case for me despite diligent effort. I looked in all the right educational places for this noticeable power of personality I desired in greater measure. I believed that I could somehow cultivate this power of personality through conforming to the mores and discipline of my chosen profession. I especially concentrated on the self-study of leadership material. I eventually earned a master's degree in organizational development. Yet that third source of power I'll call **Charisma Power** continued to elude me.

This power was an aspect of every attractive personality I was drawn toward. I have come to understand over time that all three of these sources of power are gifts from God.

There is a created supernatural being, Satan, who tries to imitate God. I have found him to be quite real. He has the ability to give false gifts to detour you from your path of destiny. If he tempted Jesus, God's only Son, in His 40-day desert experience after His baptism in the Spirit at the Jordon River, he can tempt you. A true soldier never lets down his guard, and I am still learning how to be on guard. Ultimately dependence on the wrong source of power leads to death.

Hidden treasure is available in the holy Scriptures for the man who seeks God's full truth with all his heart.

He will find who seeks truth diligently. That's a firm promise in Scripture. The men who turn to the sacred word and won't compromise, are ultimately provided with the fullness of His life. Whether in or out of the military there is a special anointing for those who seek the true source with their whole heart. What I searched for, through so many years of growing frustration, was the gift of anointing for God's purposes that comes upon His servants. I was trying to get the "what"(the right stuff). I should have been spending time seeking the "Who." The right "who" gives all the necessary "whats."

The ones who learn early this hidden source of power are those who receive mentoring by being open and eager. The only other way to pick it up is through the diligent study of Scripture with an open heart.

There are noteworthy men of achievement in our armed forces who have a strong faith in Jesus Christ. Our world system provides a definite restraint against sharing this vital internal key with others. This is a major reason I have written this book: to encourage the idealistic who feel quite alone. Our flesh wants to keep this knowledge private even where our heart cries to share this secret with another who might need such encouragement.

In the Gospel of John, God makes an important promise. He will mentor those who show a special level of moral obedience. "He who obeys the commandments he has from me is the man who loves me; and he who loves me will be loved by my father. I too will love him and reveal myself to him (John 14:21)." A good exercise is to meditate on what Jesus means by the word "reveal."

THE BAPTISM OF FIRE

In John, Chapter three, Jesus had an important conversation with a wise man in Israel, Nicodemus. That conversation is equally important for us. John the Baptist spoke of a "fire" baptism in the preceding gospels before the Book of John: "I baptize you in water...He it is who will baptize you in the Holy Ghost and fire (Matthew 3:11)." Throughout the Book of Acts, God declares the importance of two additional baptisms. The present day civilian church has not always seen the importance of these baptisms.

The church has an even more powerful weapon than the natural weapons at the disposal of the Corps according to 1 Cor. 10: 3-5. I, as a military man, appreciate what the church has to offer me and would not think of rewriting God's Word. Yet there are civilians with no clue trying to rewrite the Guide Book for Marines to effect undesireable change in our tight-knit society. They have almost destroyed the discipline within family throughout American society. Yet we still do not see the attack of the enemy from within.

Civilians may grasp the importance of influencing the armed forces environment morally by assigned chaplains to military units. Very few civilians understand the connection between a moral military and the quality of life of the civilian church. Why doesn't the civilian church stand against a sin like homosexuality with the resolve a military force must show in accomplishing its assigned combat mission in the face of a threatening evil?

If history is any judge we can expect our military society to be further eroded morally through civilian political compromise and coercion. After all look at the civilian institutions which have opened the door to homosexuality. It is no longer politically correct to be a public Christian. So, the moral climate in troop units can probably be expected to continue downward in terms of mean-spiritedness and rebellion where strong leadership is absent. It will in the future become far more difficult for moral leadership to influence organizational life in a positive, healthy way. There could come a point where the only moral restraint on individuals will be his or her private conscience from lessons learned in the home before enlisting. If that time comes what a terrible time it will be in America. Service members will face one-on-one encounters with militants from the other side of the moral spectrum in value neutral organizations where all kinds of perverse spirits have official sanctioning. That time is coming for all societies who hate God's people, Israel, according to Scripture. That is why God desires that we learn to operate in the same power Jesus and other mighty men of God operated in as recorded in the scriptural accounts. We can't do as the Word of God so clearly says to do--"Walk by faith, not by sight (2 Corinthians 5:7)"-- if we are not open to the additional baptismal experiences every fighting man needs before a good commanding officer orders him into a battle. The power to make a difference in a firefight is not available to a double-minded man.

John the Baptist strongly declared that Jesus would be the baptizer in fire and the Holy Spirit. These are two significant experiences which are only available to the person who is really willing to press in to the Lord's training for his life.

A wise sage named Saint Augustine wrote, "Understanding is the reward of faith. Therefore seek not to understand that you may believe, but believe that you may understand."

King David a man after God's own heart declared in Psalm 112:1-2, "Blessed is the man who fears the Lord, who finds great delight in his commands. His children will be mighty in the land; each generation of the up-right will be blessed."

Do you want to be a man of destiny? Are you tired of trying to make it on your own? If your answer is yes, you will need to learn to accept challenge, not run from or avoid it. This takes practice. Soldiers in an army practice for combat before their generals expose them to combat. Try something new. Neither my church which I grew up to love, nor the Marine Corps ever effectively taught me the importance or necessity of a certain, critical action. I am sure they tried, but I am equally sure that each man has to discover this important truth for himself. The ultimate challenge every man must face is the act of surrendering totally to Jesus Christ. Scripture tell us clearly He is the ultimate commander over all of life's challenges. He is the Alpha and Omega, the only one who guarantees success in life. Outside his love there is no possibility of lasting peace or happiness. Jesus declared, "I have come to light a fire on the earth. How I wish the blaze were ignited (Luke 12:49)."

Joshua, one of God's mighty Old Testament men of destiny and a prefigure of Christ, said this to his men, "So now acknowledge with your whole heart and soul that not one of all the promises the Lord, your God, made to you has remained unfulfilled, every promise has been fulfilled for you, with not one single exception (Joshua 23:14)."

If you feel Joshua's assurance is not correct for your life you may be in the wrong posture. You may need to get down on your knees and do some serious reflecting. When the light floods in you need to submit. Could you be the one hindering God's promises becoming more operational in your life? We are usually our own worst enemy. Where you lack, you might need to take more responsibility, for God has made no idle promises. He doesn't know how to lie.

OATH OF ENLISTMENT

Every army has an oath of enlistment. God's army is no different. Just as in a natural army you must surrender fully to superiors in the chain of command. I never saw a Marine general fail in his duty to his men in the forward positions. I know Jesus is even more faithful. The key is not to waiver. God hates unbelief. You may have thought you declared your allegiance years ago as a child. But, where you have been deceived by Satan you must recommit. Think back over all the times you compromised your surrender through unbelief. Daily surrender and reenlistment is not too often. When was the last time you bent your knee, raised your arms high over your head, in a true act of surrender?

For most of us it's been awhile since we were really serious about growing in our faith. How do I know this? Look at how bad television and the movies are becoming. Someone is paying the fare. It must be profitable.

I've written an enlistment oath for myself, but it probably fits your situation too. Say it out loud, hands high over your head so your body feels like it is real surrender. The angels and demons need to know clearly where you stand. The daily struggle becomes easier with God's reinforcing help. Without His help you are lost. Your present situation may seem OK, but God can make it better. Repeat this oath with sincerity and purpose then begin submitting when God's reinforcing help starts arriving. Know with certainty that you will begin to realize God has stepped into your corner in a whole new way.

Repeat this oath:

"Heavenly Father! You know me well. I've tried on my own. Compared to what I expected to accomplish, I have failed miserably. In the process of living my life I have hurt others. Even those I love the most.

Lord! I surrender to you just as I am, a miserable sinner. I have tried on my own and failed badly. I ask you now to become the Lord of my life 24 hours each day for the remainder of my life. I recognize you Jesus, as my personal Savior, as my Lord, as my Redeemer, as my Righteousness, as my Partner in every aspect of my new life. I praise the blood covenant that you entered into with me at Calvary when you paid the penalty for my transgressions. I ask for forgiveness. I forgive all those who have hurt me.

In particular I forgive_____. (Name those against whom you have harbored ill will in the recent and distant past. Take some time here.)

Lord, I ask you to send the Holy Spirit to comfort me, heal me, teach me, pray for me. Guide and assist me to always walk on your straight and narrow path in a way that is pleasing to you all the days of my life. I truly need the help of the special mentor that you promised to send to all who request His services...for I have no human mentor I can really count on for help with every problem.

I rejoice now that you have heard my heartfelt prayer and that I am one of your newly born children. I thank you that I have received a new nature from above as Jesus taught in John 3:3.

I thank you that you are sending me the fruit of life in the Holy Spirit: love, joy, peace, patient endurance, kindness, generosity, faith, mildness, and chastity. I praise you and thank you Lord, that in Him who is the source of my strength, I have strength for every task and good thing you set before me from now on.

Protect me Lord. Protect those you have given me responsibility over. Show me what I need to know, Lord. I want to come up to speed quickly so that I can serve

you with all my might. Equip me to break the bond of
bad habits that presently enslave my old nature. Otherwise they will keep me from doing my best in the future
as they so often did in the past. I specifically repent of
_____ (take time here).
Send your family here on earth across my path.
Empower them to set the right example at the right time.
Take people out of my life that hold me back from more
fully pleasing you or change them Lord. Give me the
courage to distance myself from those who don't please
you who won't be influenced.

In the name of your precious son, Jesus Christ, I voice
this prayer to you, Heavenly Father. Make yourself more
real to me so that I can truly say you are Abba, Daddy.
Thank you for inducting me into your disciplined troop
of believers this day. I voice this prayer before your host
in heaven aloud in Jesus' strong name. Amen!"

If you prayed that prayer asking Jesus to forgive you,
to become your Savior and Lord, Scripture says you have
a new spiritual nature. You may feel no difference this
very moment. But I assure you, if your heart was really
in this confession, others will soon see a difference. God
will make you a better person (the role of a drill instructor), more able to do your duty in a solid way under
whatever pressures come.

For now, keep quiet about the oath you have taken.
You may want to share your excitement with a loved
one as you begin to see you really are brand new. But
Scripture says, "Even zeal is not good when it runs ahead
of knowledge (Proverbs 19:21)." You need special tutoring first. You will receive special tutoring from the
Holy Spirit as you read His Word. He will become your
personal mentor in a whole new way. He will quicken
your spirit where you need to hang on to a special verse.
Because of your oath of surrender you no longer have

the tainted blood of Adam flowing through you. Now it's the blood of Jesus which has joined you in a new and better covenant. You will begin to see things spiritually you never saw before.

God will have to deprogram you from some character defects associated with the old nature which will fight you to hang on. But it's the commander's responsibility to change you from civilian to soldier, not yours. Your responsibility is simply to learn to hear His voice and respond to it as an obedient soldier/recruit. He will give you the training you need. He will put tutors in your path. Don't be impatient or get discouraged by your slow progress, i.e. securing the high ground. Overcoming negative personal habits entrenched in your old nature takes time. You will need to learn how to accomplish tasks assigned you. But, as with any general he first wants to be sure you really are a soldier and no longer have any bad civilian habits that could get you or others wounded, even killed. Be especially careful how you share your experience with a family member who has not received the new birth. They may not share your excitement. Pressing a loved one to see your new truth will even hurt, maybe even kill your relationship, so be cautious. Timing is everything.

Remember, Jesus Christ is the baptizer in the New Birth. No civilian wants to become a soldier unless he feels called to the life. As for you life will now begin to take on an excitement you never experienced and weren't even sure was possible. It will be full of adventure of a kind no civilian can ever know or fully appreciate. So hang on!

THE FULL ARMOR

Marines are taught in military classes the identity/characteristics of the enemy they oppose. They must be able to recognize and separate the enemy quickly from the innocent. Knowing who a soldier can fire his weapon at is critical to combat success. It is interesting to note that Marine Corps training does not spend the bulk of its training time on studying the enemy, his strengths and weaknesses. It's actually a small amount of the total training for the average soldier. The main amount of time is spent on enhancing the individual fighting skills of the soldier and promoting teamwork. That is the way it should be also with your spiritual training. Keep on track and in balance.

Spiritually speaking, who is our enemy? The Scriptures indicate very clearly that our fellow man is not our enemy. Dark forces in the spiritual realm are the real foe. To "beef up" spiritually and get into the proper condition to ward off fear, spiritual fatigue and lethargy, it's necessary to assimilate the following data.

For a Marine to be completely protected he must also arm himself against the assaults of the dark spiritual forces. The Scriptures teach us just how to accomplish this task. In the Book of Ephesians, for instance the Apostle Paul writes about putting on spiritual body armor. Do this daily! This regimen serves to strengthen you, lessening the effects of fear and deception. Over time you will understand better how Jesus is your strong tower as Scripture talks about.

"Finally, draw your strength from the Lord and His mighty power. Put on the armor of God so that you may be able to stand firm against the tactics of the devil. Our battle is not against human forces but against the principalities and powers, the rulers of this world of darkness, the evil spirits in regions above. You must put on the armor of God if you are to resist on the evil day; do all that your duty requires and hold your ground stand fast, with the truth as the belt around your waist, justice as your breastplate, and zeal to propagate the gospel of peace as your footgear. In all circumstances hold faith up before you as your shield; it will help you extinguish the fiery darts of the evil one. Take the helmet of salvation and the sword of the Spirit, the Word of God (Ephesians 6:10-18)."

COMBAT TIPS: FRESH INSIGHT TO WHET YOUR APPETITE

God's Guidebook for Soldiers, the Bible, clearly indicates in the Book of Hosea 4:6, "My people perish for lack of knowledge." This is a very strong statement. You can die before your appointed time. Learn spiritually how to dodge the fiery darts not particularly meant for you. We encounter these darts by unintentionally zigging when we should have zagged.

The Bible says, "The righteous man lives seventy years, eighty years if he is strong (Psalm 90:10)." In the book of Genesis it alludes that God has shortened the life of spiritually aware men to 120 years. It should be possible in the grace of God to live that long in his favor and strength. We'll find this in the final generation of mankind that many saints believe we are now in.

Why do some obviously good men die young? There are some answers. This quotation from 2 Maccabees, though not considered Scripture by non-Catholic traditions, indicates hidden sin and its consequences.

"On the following day, since the task had now become urgent, Judas and his men went to gather up the bodies of the slain and bury them with their kinsmen in their ancestral tombs. But under the tunic of each of the dead they found amulets sacred to the idols of Jamnia, which the law forbids the Jews to wear. So it was clear to all that this was why these men had been slain. They all therefore praised the ways of the Lord, the just judge who brings to light the things that are hidden (2

Maccabees 12:39-41)." (This Jewish wisdom book is found in the Protestant Apocrypha collection available in Bible book stores and included in the Catholic Bible.)

The second interesting combat tip from the aprocryphal Book of Wisdom has helped a lot of Vietnam veterans who made it safely home after the war but suffer from what some call survivor's guilt. They had friends who died. They knew in their hearts that the friend or friends who died were better men morally. So how is this explained?

"But the just man, though he die early, shall be at rest...He who pleased God was loved. He who lived among sinners was transported-snatched away, lest wickedness pervert his mind or deceit beguile his soul; for the witchery of paltry things obscures what is right and the whirl of desire transforms the innocent mind. Having become perfect in a short while, he reached the fullness of a long career; for his soul was pleasing to the Lord, therefore he sped him out of the midst of wickedness. But the people saw and did not understand, nor did they take this into account. Yes, the just man dead condemns the sinful who live, and youth swiftly completed condemns the many years of the wicked man grown old. For they see the death of the wise man and do not understand what the Lord intended for him, or why he made him secure. They see, and hold him in contempt; but the Lord laughs them to scorn. And they shall afterward become dishonored corpses and an unceasing mockery among the dead, For he shall strike them down speechless and prostrate and rock them to their foundations; they shall be utterly laid waste and shall be in grief and their memory shall perish...(Book of Wisdom 4: 7, 10-19)."

SOLDIER'S BRAWLS ARE FORGOTTEN WHEN THE REAL ENEMY ATTACKS

There is more agreement between the two halves of the Christian world, Protestant and Catholic (those who open their spiritual eyes find believers in both religious institutions), than the non-Christian world could ever imagine from the cat and dog fights that are such a spectacle to many inside and outside of the body of Christ. There are a lot of arguments, fighting, and sometimes even terrible misunderstandings between these two belief systems that both say they honor Jesus Christ. If more believers could see the larger Christian world as more of an all-encompassing Department of Defense, made up of various branches of fighting forces like the army, navy, air force, coast guard, and Marine Corps, I wonder if they would be more tolerant towards interpretations of Scripture made in good faith that they consider alien?

Why has God allowed the diversity to exist between different Christian worlds? Shouldn't we be focusing on what we do agree on? For instance biggies like the trinity and the divinity of Jesus Christ and the role of the Holy Spirit? At the top of the various organizational chains of command are pastoral leaders who have all sworn allegiance to the same Commanding General, Jesus Christ. Isn't He the one who has allowed all the organizational diversity within His Department of Defense? Maybe we need to spend less time arguing over the variations in our daily routines (doctrines) and begin to recognize that we are, in fact, submitted to the same spiritual authority at the top and get on with the main job of defeating the real enemy. There is a real enemy more important than those you see as denominational foes.

Because we can't judge as God does with total understanding, some say don't judge at all. But with the Scriptures to point the way and time spent dialoguing and in fellowship, we can pretty well determine whether one is walking on the broad path or the narrow path. Whichever path one is on (see illustration page 197), that is the path of his choice in terms of the objectives He wants to accomplish for his life. The Bible is very clear that the final destiny for one who stays on the "broad path" is destruction, and the second death. It's the "narrow path" that leads to life and eternal salvation that we want to cross the finish line on. Your example will influence more than merely what you say.

We could debate into the wee hours of the morning the final fate of Lt. Col. Pete Ellis and General John Lejeune though they were on the same earthly team in very important ways. We will not know for sure whether one or both crossed that final finish line until we cross into eternity ourselves.

One thing is for sure. We will all experience death once. It's the second death spoken about clearly in the Book of Revelation that we don't want to experience. The bottom line — life — is what this book is all about. One major difference between soldiers and civilians is that soldiers are forced by their oath, training, and mission to consider the real possibility of death or injury more seriously.

My father long ago shared an old saying with me, "You will find no atheists in the foxholes in combat zones." In spite of the difference between John Lejeune and Pete Ellis in terms of their off-duty behavior, the result of a different understanding of spiritual reality, they loved each other in a brotherly way. Their love transcended their spiritual differences allowing them to accomplish something beyond the capability of either to accomplish alone. That is the kind of love that is needed in a combat brotherhood. Members need real unity to accomplish their unit mission in war. A brother who operates on this level of power in his unit will make a huge difference in the lives of those around him as he goes about doing what soldiers have been prepared to do. An important question is: which path are you on right now? No one knows his appointed time to die. So, today is the day to make sure you're on the right path.

God willing, both men of destiny I highlighted in chapter six will be there to meet me when I cross the finish line into eternity. With God's continued grace I know I will cross that line. I believe in my heart John Lejeune among others was prompted to intercede in prayer for Pete Ellis in that critical moment when he had his last chance for surrender before entering eternity. I know through experience the power of prayer to influence a sinner's soul during the critical final moments is real. But surrender is vital, as God honors free will. So, I won't know until the next life whether the general interceded in prayer or whether the Lt. Colonel responded by crying out to the Lord (Jude 20).

I have immense respect for these men's worldly accomplishments. Few can expect to reach the level of fame of either of these men here on earth. I know which man was the better role model for me. How one uses his free time is a vital day-to-day choice. Who we chose to hang out with and emulate can be a life or death matter. I hope Pete surrendered in the final moments of his life. I hope he recognized the gravity of his final situation. I hope he called out to the only one who is faithful and able to deliver from desperate situations, like imminent death.

From my research it seems obvious John Lejeune had a safer set of morals for such a tough moment. I doubt he was ever out of control through drunkenness. Both were warriors in a worldly sense. But the real key to life is not "what" you know, but in the final analysis it's "who" you know that counts. God does not want puppets in heaven. He honors free will even when it means choosing hell for all eternity.

Are you certain what your final cry would be? Who will you cry out to when the angel of death is knocking? Will that be a moment of desperation and terror? Will habits practiced in life lock you in or out? Your final moments should be full of joy-filled expectancy! Death comes in an instant and eternity is forever! The wicked are unprepared for it. When your turn comes, don't be with the wrong crowd!

The first hands to touch me in this life were those of a Chinese doctor. I was an alien in a foreign land. The only hands to touch me in the new life in Jesus Christ are hands permitted by the Lord God Almighty. I have chosen the narrow path that leads to life. At times it seems more difficult, the longer way around. But then I consider the final destiny of those on the broad path. It is with certainty the easier path to be on until the ambush comes. You choose your final destiny. The great adventure is on the path the crowd avoids. Why be a civilian when you can be a soldier like Christ?

Today I saw the bravest man I have ever known and I know He was brave because I was attempting to stand right next to Him, and I know He died on the cross for me.

The final chapter discusses the critical importance of locating and rejecting "sin from the camp" so success won't be hampered. Sin, and the need for repentence, are highly emotional topics. Sin causes polarization. Polarization can't be tolerated in an organization where life or death revolves around the level of unity (the principle of mass). Sin must be addressed not because I want to address it, but because spokesmen for perverted lifestyles have targeted the armed forces of the United

States of America as a battleground to force their agenda. They want no less than the complete surrender of the people of our nation to their point of view. I feel badly for those caught up in death styles.

Men who chose styles of living that lead to early death, have too often been ambushed by drugs, alcohol and illicit sexual relationships. They are to be pitied for choosing to remain in such obvious forms of escape from reality. But in a military force where survival is the goal, loved ones are the major concern. Don't skip this last chapter because it is a sensitive topic. The one who sees the value of forsaking the civilian life for the life of a combat soldier by beginning to speak out his or her true convictions will begin to make a real difference in the lives of others.

"I have set before you life and death,
blessings and curses. Now
choose life,
so that you and your children may live..."

"...*Love* the Lord your God,
listen to his voice, and
hold fast to him.

For the *Lord* is your *life*."
Deut. 30:19b-20a

SIN IN THE CAMP

"...they did not abandon their practices or their stubborn ways. So the anger of the Lord burned against Israel, and He said, 'Because this nation has transgressed my covenant which I commanded their fathers, and has not listened to My voice, I also will no longer drive out before them any of the nations which Joshua left when he died.' "
Judges 2: 19b, 20, 21

How did we allow the sin of homosexuality into the military camps that defend our nation?

How did America reach the point of such moral decline that in 1993 the president of the United States signed an administrative edict making homosexual behavior an acceptable practice within the Department of Defense? The reason is "silence."

Too many Americans hesitate to take a firm stand on such controversial matters in social settings like public schools, churches, and places of work because they are not intellectually prepared to take stands. This is the reason for silence by most Americans. What the majority believes collectively concerning homosexuality is no secret. However, most remain silent because they fear standing alone on public issues in spheres of influence. We don't want to make fools of ourselves.

The bold propaganda campaign the mass media wages on TV, Hollywood movies, art, and printed literature has a direct emphasis on "political correctness." Most academic circles have also taken a liberal stand to be politically correct.

The power elite's bold, largely distorted stand on this issue confuses the majority. The majority wants to believe in, honor, and respect the power elite. This has been our tradition. In the past where the Judeo-Christian ethic had a stronger influence they could be trusted— this is tragically no longer the case. Secular humanism is now the ruling ethic of the day. Outside certain hot talk radio listening circles the Silent Majority is disturbingly quiet, some might say gutless. "Moral confusion" on the homosexuality issue in the light of the true facts is disappointing for those who want to speak out but feel so alone.

Homosexuality has been mostly a hidden practice for thousands of years, outlawed behavior by most peoples. Historically, where this behavior reached any level of social respectability it was in the very final stages of that civilization's messy breakup. Has America crossed the line? Have we gone beyond the point of no return? Perhaps.

There seems to still be some hope for America on this issue. In spite of this blatant presidential attempt to institutionally sodomize our military, this practice is still widely despised by the majority according to American Gallup polls. It was encouraging to see a number of political leaders boldly stand against this 1993 presidential action. Their public opposition lessened the edict's negative effect, thank God. However, we must stay vigilant.

Is "gutless" an accurate description of those who are silent? I don't think so. I do not believe the majority is gutless. I think they simply err on the side of politeness. They don't want to let go of their belief in the supremacy of civilized behavior. Liberals do a great job faking civilized behavior. Don't be fooled. If you are not armed well enough with the true facts to pleasantly disagree, do your research. Become verbally armed.

It may be difficult wading through the overwhelming amount of myth, misinformation, and misunderstanding concerning this issue. But make the effort anyway to get at the true facts. Don't expect the truth to receive equal time in mass media outlets. Too few in the majority trust their gut feelings enough to wade into controversial issues without intellectual facts, but the militants on the other side of controversial matters are well prepared and have smooth tongues. You must be as prepared, if not more so, as those whom you oppose.

We all want to be correct, right, and popular concerning such matters. Controversy more often scatters than draws the correct crowd. The natural tendency is to give plenty of room to anyone who makes motions to confront evil. The crowd knows such a man will draw return fire. Few are willing to be caught in the crossfire, and few are armed well enough to protect themselves during such a fight. Week after week even in pulpits across America too few pastors speak out forcefully against specific evils such as pornography, adultery, fornication, pride, no-fault divorce, R-rated movies, and the like. Most pastors seem to share many of the very same views as their fellow Americans — views of compromise.

So why should we take up the verbal sword? Why should we speak out? In reality all of life is lived in a combat zone. You may think of yourself as a civilian, not a soldier. But, the bottom line is — you serve in one army or the other. There are two: God's or Satan's. Whether or not you ever formally choose to be on one side or the other of a major controversy, by default you ultimately end up in one army or the other.

This is one of your major choices in this life — the "army life." You are according to Scripture either on the "broad path" with a very large army heading towards hell, or you are on the "narrow path" with a much smaller army marching towards heaven.

No civilians make it into Heaven. Your commanding general, whether you like it or not, is either Jesus Christ or Satan. Indecision on this point of fact will get you killed. You must choose whom you will serve!

Can you learn anything about staying alive in the combat environment called life from a study of the Old Testament? Yes! The Hebrews followed their new leader, Joshua, across the Jordon River (Joshua chapter four, verse 23). After 40 years in the wilderness desert under the able leadership of Moses, the sons and daughters of the parents who left Egypt and slavery, achieved a spectacular military success at the battle of Jericho. They took this well-fortified city in a very unnatural manner with supernatural help from God.

Now, look at chapter seven's first verse: "...and the anger of Jehovah was kindled against the children of Israel." Why did God become angry with the entire army? Because there was sin in the camp! Achan, the son of Carmi of the tribe of Judah took and hid unlawful secret items under his tent. This evil act of disobedience by one man caused the whole army to suffer. In the very next military action against the men of Ai, the Israelite's esprit de corps (spirit of unity) evaporated. This man's disobedience caused a curse to come upon the entire camp. Joshua took the appropriate action. He hunted down the domestic enemy in their midst.

This book is all about staying alive under combat conditions. Satan is a very clever enemy, our only real enemy according to Ephesians 6:11,12. Because of his nature as a liar and deceiver, I can't avoid discussing in this final chapter the highly unpopular topic of sin. In infantry terms sin is to the believer what a military objective is to the attacking force. When the military attacks it is under the direction of the commander's operation order. The operation order God gave Moses to lead his people successfully in the desert was the Ten Commandments. When there was no sin in the camp, God was out ahead of his army destroying the enemy. The only problems occurred when sin was allowed to enter the camp.

Sin causes a breech (breakdown) in the defense that Satan complained about to God in chapter one of the book of Job. Jesus Christ gives us Satan's mission statement in John chapter ten, verse ten: "The thief comes to steal and kill and destroy." Isn't it interesting that this is the official army mission statement for a combat infantry unit?

Since the church seems so powerless today in standing against the advance of the tide of evil, what is the problem? The obvious answer must be "sin in the camp." The opening quote in this chapter from the Book of Judges is timeless. America has the very same sin problem today. We have become stubborn and disobedient. We have refused to abandon our practices — the practices that God abhors. I fear that He will soon not be willing to drive out the very enemies of sin that I am writing about here.

Military Polarization

In the interest of not polarizing the armed forces (or churches) few military leaders (all military leaders are in reality pastors) today make bold, open comments on moral issues such as Joshua made in chapter one of the book of his life. So the type of polarization now occuring in the larger civilian society is destined for most military units. We have a growing problem in the military because we serve an increasingly mixed-up group of civilians. Privately, knowledgeable military leaders are alarmed with this turn of events. They see America's fighting capability increasingly weakened by ignorant civilian tampering with long held institutional restraints that work.

I want to make a strong statement. There are many ills in society that are a growing plague within the military. Homosexuality is only one of them. We live in a world today where lust of all kinds and unspeakable immorality is dictated as the norm. And as it goes in civilian society, so it goes in the military. Allow me to use the following Scripture segment to focus my point:

"Wherefore God gave them up in the lusts of their hearts unto uncleanness, that their bodies should be dishonored among themselves: for that they exchanged the truth of God for a lie, and worshipped and served the creature rather than the Creator, who is blessed forever. Amen. For this cause God gave them up unto vile passions; for their women changed the natural use into that which is against nature: and likewise also the men, leaving the natural use of the woman, burned in their lust one toward another, men with men working unseemliness, and receiving in themselves that recompense of their error which was due. And even as they refused to have God in their knowledge, God gave them up unto a reprobate mind, to do those things which are not fitting; being filled with all unrighteousness, wickedness, covetousness, maliciousness; full of envy, murder, strife, deceit, malignity; whisperers, backbiters, hateful to God, insolent, haughty, boastful, inventors of evil things, disobedient to parents, without understanding, covenant-breakers, without natural affection, unmerciful: who, knowing the ordinance of God, that they that practise such things are worthy of death, not only do the same, but also consent with them that practise them (Romans 1:24-32)."

Many legislative and legal actions have been taken since WW II by civilian leadership that have adversely impacted military society. I will address just two such national restraints that were lifted with widespread chaos inside the military. These are restraints concerning divorce and the complete ban on homosexual practices. As with civilian society, "The wicked are increasingly strutting about because what is vile is being honored among men." Removing restraints against certain human behavior allows freedom for the wicked to strut about. The military can ill afford such behavior within its tight-knit society which can't afford polarization over such controversial topics.

God considers divorce a "vile thing." Jesus was often asked about divorce. He never gave a popular answer. He said, "Because of the hardness of your hearts Moses permitted divorce, but in the beginning it was not so (Matthew 19:8)." He took his disciples back to the beginning when he said, "The two shall become one flesh (Mt. 10:8)." Marriage is a covenant made before God. God has very unpopular things to say about holding to a vow once taken. He says to be very cautious about taking any vow. If you take a vow whether the military oath of enlistment or a marriage vow he will expect you to keep your vow (Romans 14:12).

How can civilian society pass a law that makes it universally easy for one party to break a solemn vow like the marriage vow without expecting that it will have ramifications? Consider the impact upon those like Michael New, who treat seriously the military oath of enlistment? For me divorce is to marriage what desertion is to an army. Within six months of returning home to the new no-fault divorce environment from Vietnam, 36 percent of war veterans experienced divorce. Many would not have volunteered for war if they had known it would have such an impact on their family upon their return home. The same thing happened to Desert Storm veterans. Over 92 percent of Vietnam veterans have been divorced at least once since Vietnam. In light of their unselfish contribution to their nation, divorce has caused veterans great and unfair pain in the aftermath of their war experience. It has devasted far too many children of Vietnam veterans.

NO-FAULT DIVORCE AT FAULT

Divorce is a vile thing. No-fault divorce is a very wrong public policy. Today in America it is easier to get out of a marriage than it is to get out of a contract to buy a refrigerator, car, or home. When an adult breaks a contract to buy a car the dealership can sue the defaulting buyer for specific performance, and vice versa; not so with the marriage contract in America.

If a veteran wants to honor his marriage vows, no-fault divorce is a violation of his right of due process guaranteed by the very Constitution he has sworn to uphold. It only takes one party to break the marriage contract. This is not right. Too many spouses desire with all their heart to restore the marriage, yet have no chance to do so. The divorcing party can serve the papers on the other party. As long as he or she gets a copy the divorce is finalized even though the other party refuses to sign in protest. The party who may want to save the marriage for the sake of children or out of religious conviction has no right to stop the divorce even where he or she is quite innocent of any wrongdoing.

Though the United States Constitution guarantees the right of "due process" all 50 of our states have looked the other way, denying veterans their right of due process in this important matter. No-fault divorce would probably not be considered a vile thing next to homosexual behavior. But certainly one weakens resolve against the other. I personally know children and ex-spouses badly hurt by society because it sided unilaterally with the parent who wanted a divorce, too often for selfish reasons. Any long-term marriage has periods of time where one spouse or the other will be up or down in commitment to their marriage vow. It is a vile thing for the state to always side with the party wanting a divorce with no blame placed. Many vile practices are entered into by the majority because of the spirit of compromise rampant across America. With the increasing level of "vileness" is it not obvious why the wicked increasingly feel free to strut about?

CONVICTIONS

This is not a politically correct chapter. It is a chapter more about having the courage of your convictions than about any one kind of wrong behavior. That makes it unpopular and not politically correct from a liberal's point of view. But I cannot remain silent about the things I feel so strongly about. Silence where evil is on the move is consent. Silence too often is cowardly behavior. Cowardice is not what being a good soldier is all about. This is my conviction.

History can be viewed as the record of bullies in leadership positions using raw power to obtain what can not be obtained by legitimate mandate from the majority. The United States has been a unique exception to this bullying tactic for most of our short history. We were designed to be a republic. Sadly we have now regressed to the status of a democracy. To date no democracy has ever lasted longer than 200 years in the march of time. Alexander Fraser Tyler (1748-1813) wrote a remarkable book about ancient democracy: The Decline and Fall of the Athenian Republic. In the following quote, note the 200 year reference:

> "A democracy cannot exist as the permanent form of government. It can only exist until the voters discover they can vote themselves money from the public treasury. From that moment on the majority always votes for the candidates promising the most benefits from the public treasury with a result that a democracy always collapses over loose fiscal policy always followed by dictatorship. The average age of the world's greatest civilizations has been 200 years. These nations have progressed through the following sequence: from bondage to spiritual faith, from spiritual faith to great courage, from courage to liberty, from liberty to abundance, from abundance to selfishness, from selfishness to complacency, from complacency to apathy, from apathy to dependency, from dependency back into bondage."

Where is the United States in this cycle? In the light of current events we appear to be nearing the end. Can we turn our country around? Thank God for the right of free speech. We have not yet reached the tyranny of the minority. But critics of my point of view do control obvious power positions in the press, universities, and an increasing number of churches. My point of view is considered "homophobic." An unreasonable fear of homosexuality is a growing baseball bat. Should I really care what my critics think with Jesus supporting my view? He is the author of the whole Bible, His personal testimony says so. In John 17 he said that they who hated him will hate me (his disciples) also. In the present democratic process I have as much right to my opinion as a militant homosexual or his supporters have to theirs. So, I will devote the remainder of this chapter to arming you with real facts, not their myths and half-truths. The very survival of our nation depends on a healthy national debate so that the opinion of Jesus Christ will prevail.

ARMING YOURSELF

There is such a thing as the power of righteous anger. Those holding perverted views of life hide deep personal insecurities. I get no joy from speaking the truth when it hurts others. I feel only grief. But individuals who place themselves in the spotlight to legitimize perverted thinking as an alternative to repenting of their wrong behavior, should not expect you or me to stand quietly by. What they are attempting to do may be legalized by the ignorant. But you must never legitimize such behavior in your mind or heart.

This lifestyle is a result of character weakness in the adult population. Few practicioners get to the level of confirmed sodomy without first dabbling in lesser forms of perversion (rebellion against the norms of the majority). My heart aches for a young, innocent child who has been victimized (sodomized) by an adult he or she should have been able to trust. Incest is a terrible thing. In a general sense the majority is to blame for letting such things happen. But that is not a reason to cave in to the unreasonable demands by an obvious minority. It is a sad commentary on American life that this issue is important politically.

This is a life or death issue for our society. As an officer of the United States commissioned by Congress, I have taken a sworn oath to defend against all enemies, even domestic ones. We are increasingly seeing wicked citizens strutting about among us. The question is, are we going to do something about it?

The first step is the importance of a general call to repentance inside the church. We are all guilty to some degree of practicing vileness. We need to shore up our internal defenses. How can the church be a light to the world in stopping greater evils before learning how to stop lesser evils inside our body? Are enough of us willing to give up what is vile and honor a purer style of living so that worse evils in society, such as bestiality, can be dealt with effectively? If we are not willing to get our own lives straightened out so we in good conscience can speak out in our arena of influence, America will shortly disintegrate as did the Athenian Empire.

Lifting the ban on forbidding homosexuals to openly practice in the military will open the door wider to a death sentence for Western society. God never tolerates such behavior for long. An excerpt from retired U.S. Army Chaplain, Colonel E. H. Ammerman's chaplaincy letter of January 29, 1993 to President Bill Clinton is worth our attention:

Homosexuals in the U.S. Military would do more than just undermine discipline and morale, although they would do that as well.

Homosexuals are notoriously promiscuous. Most have dozens of partners, with many boasting of over 300 in a lifetime. They are also perverted, as we find repeatedly announced in the news, going for the young - pedophiles. They are aggressive recruiters for their sexual lifestyle, especially for the young. Leaders in the military exercise a far greater degree of control over their subordinates than do civilians. "The expressed desire" of a military leader is tantamount to an order. What would a homosexual leader do to his/her followers? In civilian life, one may work with a homosexual, then return to the home for one's own preferred lifestyle. Not so for the soldier who often must eat, work, sleep and shower with others. They live with little privacy, especially in the field or aboard ship. Should they be required to do so with someone lusting after them? The military is oriented toward ultimate combat, if need be. They are required to give first aid to injured comrades, whose body fluids may be spilling out, without benefit of latex gloves or other prophylactics. The military life places innocent soldiers in jeopardy of life and health enough already, without adding the heightened prospect of HIV via serving homosexuals.

It is difficult to imagine how much more the state of readiness in America will fall if the homosexual ban is lifted even further.

Never has the Department of Defense faced a more severe challenge than the lifting of this ban. Napoleon, one of the great generals of history, made the much studied point that: "The moral is to the physical as three to one." Napoleon conveyed to his troops with these ten telling words that correct morals are three times greater a contribution to the cause than a weapon's power at the men's fingertips. No general ever made the point more effectively. Moral power is the ultimate power. Sound morals are essential for the country that wishes to endure.

DON'T ASK, DON'T TELL

What are the real facts concerning homosexuals and their ability to serve? Is this really a sign of a growing specter in our land? I will elaborate on six major points made by proponents of this lifestyle. Powerful elements of the press, the church, and the universities are deceived as you will see from the true facts. You need to know they are deceived in their thinking. Ignorance, fear, and "birds of a feather who flock together" are a problem. The truth is our ally not theirs.

Learn the truth. The "don't ask, don't tell" policy hammered out by Congress in 1993 violates the clear wishes of the silent majority. It was done for political not military reasons. This administrative battle is not over unless you give up within your sphere of influence. Proper facts will arm you for verbal combat. Determine the role you wish to play in the battle of words. Even if the decision is made to lift the ban totally, the war is not lost in your arena of action unless you capitulate. The following pages are extremely vital to your well being and to the well being of your young, impressionable family members who may have to contend with elevated disinformation campaigns in their very own classrooms if the situation worsens. Compromise on this issue has eternal as well as natural consequences. Don't remain ignorant and silent, thereby allowing evil to spread further.

Leaders in the homosexual community approach this issue as a life or death matter. You must demonstrate

equal strength of conviction. Make sure your verbal box-
ing gloves are full of dynamite facts. In the best tradition of the men from Lexington and Concord, farmers
by day and soldiers once the need arose, you must be a
disciplined soldier (if in uniform) during the day, and a
concerned citizen, your right, during off-duty time. Be
toughminded. Be willing to take a hit by speaking the
truth. Know you hold the superior moral position. Your
side will prevail, the Bible says so. Prophesy clearly
shows however that we will lose important tactical skir-
mishes in the future.

Believe God's word on this subject. Don't be concerned with how few are willing to defend the truth. It's
always that way. The initial stages of any great debate
are lonely ones for truth-tellers. And this is a great debate; in my view equal to the debate over slavery in the
last century.

Doctor Mallory, a psychiatrist and director of the
Atlanta Counseling Center presented this interesting
analogy: "A physician would be guilty of malpractice if
he didn't warn a person carrying a disease of his condition because he didn't want to hurt his feeling."

Too often representatives in Congress cave on key
battles because of a lack of character. Troops may have
to confront homosexuals and lesbians in their very midst
because of civilian cowardness. Mostly generals don't
win important battles, courageous troops do.

The homosexual lifestyle is not just abnormal, but
life threatening for them as well as for you. You are doing them a favor by taking a stand for the truth. If real
facts are made known they will keep this movement from
growing. The truth can even help deliver poor souls out
of this unsatisfactory choice of lifestyle. Shame, however,
must be free to do its liberating work. Effective witnessing can't be done in a "condemning spirit." Emotion is
useless where unsupported with intelligent facts. Genu-

ine concern must be demonstrated for the facts. This can only be accomplished by understanding the true depravity associated with such sex. You can't act from a spirit of fear. Compassionate intelligence must be the order of the day. The truly tough man demonstrates mercy where appropriate. A real man doesn't have to retaliate with below-the-belt tactics just because they might be used by the other side. Name calling or hostile body language only elicits sympathy for those attacked in such a manner. By knowing the truth you can maintain the moral high ground. Truth is your overwhelming advantage, even where you are compromised politically.

Six myths are looked upon as truth by many in the mainstream media. They are too often the frontline attack for this deceptive and distorted message.

THE SIX MYTHS OF THE HOMOSEXUAL LOBBY

MYTH #1. "One out of every ten Americans is homosexual."

This is a lie! This statistic is quoted constantly. Most who use this statistic faithfully don't even know its only source, a highly flawed report published in 1948 by William Kinsey. No study since has ever substantiated his statistic. Kinsey's methodology was highly flawed. Twenty-five percent of the 5300 studied were prison inmates who had no opportunity for normal sex. Forty-four percent of the inmates had their homosexual contacts while in prison. Certainly they were not representative of the normal American population. Also, several hundred male prostitutes were used further distorting its findings. Another major flaw was his sampling. It was done on a volunteer basis generated by ads run in a newspaper. All who responded were accepted. Those who use this study don't quote it accurately. Even with all these flaws the hardened homosexual rate was still only 4 percent. All the studies since have put the actual statistic in a range of between .7 percent and 1.7 percent, a far cry from 10 percent.

MYTH #2. " Homosexuals are born that way."

The inference is that if the homosexual is simply following his genes then ultimately he cannot be considered immoral or unnatural. I like what Congressman William Dennemeyer says about this: "If homosexuality is a perversion of what is natural, then homosexuals must look at their own conduct in an entirely different light and explain it in less satisfying terms."

There is no serious scientist who buys into the biological theory that the homosexual was born that way. The recent research in the area of brain size differences has been scientifically refuted. The second factor often discussed is the environmental factor. More psychiatrists believe homosexuality arises from various environmental factors. Most say the root causes are psychological, not biological. Most homosexuals want desperately to believe that they are born that way and had no choice in their sexual preference. But the most respected professionals deny that this is caused by biological factors. There is growing evidence that much of this preference is passed on and acquired through the violence of incest or rape be it physical, emotional, psychological, or spiritual. Therapists helping homosexuals recite case after case of unhappy homosexuals who had negative childhood experiences. They were raised in very unhappy circumstances, never knowing real love and acceptance. The child's reaction to such lack of nurturing and rejection is often formulated before five years of age. Robert Kronemeyer in *Overcoming Homosexuality* writes "In 25 years of experience I firmly believe homosexuality is a learned response to early painful experience and that it can be unlearned by those who are unhappy with this life and seek effective theraphy."

MYTH #3. "Homosexuals are normal."

This is a universal contention of homosexuals. They dogmatically state that all competent psychiatrists and psychologists agree. Yet when you study the American Psychiatric Association's highly controversial decision, often quoted as justification for their claim, you see that the APA was "battered" and "bruised" into submission. Gay activists used forged credentials to gain access to APA annual conventions over a three-year period. Scare tactics, threats, and intimidation accomplished what discussion could not. When the trustees made the decision to avoid further confrontation large numbers quit the APA in disgust. Militant homosexuals attacked any APA member who dared to present any findings adverse to their movement. The APA trustee's decision was called "The medical hoax of the century," according to Dr. Paul Cameron of the Family Research Institute.

MYTH #4. "It's a healthy lifestyle."

While the gay spokesmen are constantly stressing that it's a normal and healthy lifestyle, it's easy to show otherwise. Two areas will show this. *Homosexualities*, an official publication of the Institute of Sex Research reported only 10 percent of male homosexuals could be termed as relatively monogamous. Sixty percent had more than 250 lifetime sex partners. Twenty-eight percent, more than 1,000 partners. Seventy-nine percent admitted more than 50 percent of the partners were strangers. The average AIDS patient has had 60 different partners over the last 12 months.

In contrast the average heterosexual throughout life has from five to nine partners which surprises me because I have had only one sexual partner in my 56 years and I don't think of myself as a rare exception.

Are homosexual practices healthy? I don't mean to shock, but if you want to feel nauseous, research some of these definitions: water sports, fisting, sodomy, fellatio, Kaposi's sarcoma, or Bowen's disease. Eighty-six percent of homosexual males use drugs to enhance or encourage excitement. This tells me that the physical pleasure by itself is not enough for most practitioners. Homosexuals are three times more suicidal; seven times more likely to experience a violent death, most often at the hands of a jealous partner; their life span is 33 percent shorter, and the average confirmed homosexual dies at the age of 41 years of age (the lesbian 43 years).

MYTH #5. "Change is not possible."

Virtually all gays caught up in the lifestyle deny that change is possible. Yet, there are many who have been delivered from this bondage. They will tell you a far different story. Most psychiatrists and psychologists state that conversions are a normal part of their practice, and have occurred for decades. While it is not easy, they will tell you that it is possible. A number of Christian ministries specialize in this work with great success. Just as alcoholics, drug addicts, and those addicted to pornography can recover from their addiction, so can homosexuals from theirs.

MYTH #6. "Everyone who attacks the homosexual lifestyle is homophobic."

Homophobia denotes an irrational fear or hatred of homosexuals. The Kinsey Institute defines homophobia as "the fear, dislike or hatred of homosexuals." No one should be burdened down by irrational fear or hatred. But, certainly there are rational reasons to hate this bondage that consumes those afflicted with such a driving lust. It victimizes many additional people. I must warn you the deceived gay rights movement, as well as many in the media, church, and academic communities have bought into these half-truths promoted over the years. Their media access and educational success demonstrates clearly the power of a lie repeated often enough. Many are just too close to the problem. It brings them too much pain. Practicing homosexuals I know are nice, and often successful, people in business, church, and heterosexual social environments which makes it too easy not to see them as victims or potential victimizers. Their families who are straight too often have capitulated to their half-truths as a way to maintain peace. It is convenient to tag as a bigot anyone who opposes their homosexual agenda. The majority too often simply hates any form of personal confrontation and is willing to compromise at any cost.

It is wise for a fighter to be prepared for reverse name calling and discrimination. Those struggling with this bondage are to be pitied. But, pity all the more young partners who fall victim for the first time to this relentless lust. The statistics are powerful showing that lust-driven homosexual males are significantly more likely to abuse children than lust-driven heterosexuals. I am surprised at the number of civilian leaders who are willing to excuse these communities. Is it from ignorance, fear, or hypocrisy? I don't know. All reprobates must be held accountable for their actions whether alcoholics, pornographers, drug addicts, or those with perverted sex habits. Perverse habits that the addict does not want to let go of, not the lack of jobs, are too often at the core of our unemployment and health care problems.

I urge you to familiarize yourself with the six myths presented above so you can counter half-truths as opportunities surface.

OUTSTANDING FITNESS CRITICAL TO MILITARY SUCCESS

The military must be a healthy environment. The need for a high state of physical fitness in combat is paramount for soldiers. Physical fitness helps cut the level of fatigue in frightful circumstances. Combat circumstances leave many participants so fatigued they are drained to the point of exhaustion, even those in top physical condition. A host of sicknesses and diseases that bypass those who are normal sexually will overburden our military hospitals with the lifting of this essential ban. Aids, TB and hepatitis B will top the list of high-cost diseases we will invite into our military family unless "don't ask, don't tell" is reversed. An immoral internal attitude is the enemy of a healthy body (whether personal or organizational).

Admiral Mahan in the 19th century was quoted as saying, "The real purpose of military power is to allow time for a moral climate to take root." How can this be where our military compromises institutionally with immorality from within? It is obvious that a moral climate once again needs to take root in America. During the Roman Empire's existence, soldiers were not first-class citizens in the same way as are members of the present day armed forces of America. The teaching corps of our armed forces may be the last great bastion of traditional values in our nation. Most other institutions have been compromised or they would be coming to the aid of this attack on our Department of Defense.

Military members who refuse to compromise with evil in any form have something to offer a civilian society seemingly so out of control morally. Beyond the main gates of our military posts and stations, whether home or abroad, is growing civilian chaos.

ON THE EDGE OF COLLAPSE

Whenever a once-great nation falls, historians take a close look at the major cause for that fall. One lesson emerges from the ashes time and again. The Roman Empire is an example of a rapid regression near the end. At the time of its fall, the centurions defending it were a poor shadow of the forerunners who made that nation for over 900 years the greatest republic in history. Anyone who has studied world history knows the last Roman emperors were morally corrupt. Their edicts created chaos accelerating the empire's fall.

The after-hours moral actions of a nation's men are the reason for its initial ability to endure. The collapse of individual morals (vileness walks ahead of evil) brings about that nation's demise. Smaller nations have achieved victory over a numerically stronger neighbor with telling frequency. Do not take lightly this historical lesson. Even though we are supposedly the world's only true superpower a group of less powerful nations can be gathered to come against us. We must remain strong for this reason.

You who have had military experience are the nation's true defense experts. You know better than most civilians the historical truth concerning a nation's ability to survive. What should your role be in this present national debate? What are the best morals for governing our nation? Those morals that have at their root a spirit of sacrifice (chastity) or morals centered on pleasure seeking pursuits? Can the military afford to remain aloof from this moral debate? Many of us did when we came home from our combat tours during the Vietnam conflict where so much misinformation abounded in the civilian sector. We were naturally tired and wanted to catch up after having been deprived of a normal civilian life. But the aftermath of our silence and non-involvement was added moral confusion, chaos and worse. Ask any Vietnam veteran.

No one can learn effectively how to survive war by watching Hollywood movies depicting war or by watching TV accounts. Could the internal breakdown of our society be connected with the ending of the draft, a stupid decision in light of our present lack of discipline? Every European nation still has a draft and far less civil disobedience. Mandatory military service exposes young men to further discipline beyond their families which helps them form character. What Hollywood teaches concerning the needed character of men in combat is too often the exact opposite of why men really endure and prevail in tough times. Too often wrong personality attributes are dramatized as the movie *A Few Good Men* illustrates. Men with clean hearts and pure minds carry the major load in combat. The military force with the greatest number of men with such moral character is the side that achieves most victories. This was wonderfully illustrated in the movie *Braveheart*, a true story.

America has been praised by foreigners over the years who visited our land and marveled at the "goodness" of our people. This was in days past due to the quality of our religious upbringing. Yet key figures in powerful positions are now tampering with our historic and vital inner core, the Judeo-Christian ethic while most in the church sit quietly doing nothing. This national ethic has worked better than any ethic in history in terms of natural achievement.

There is a reason emigrants flock into and not out of our country. Will this begin to change in our lifetime? More and more Americans are starting to talk about emigrating out of this country. Most characters Hollywood exalts today emphasize the foul, the profane, and the violent. More and more American movies are an insult to the former good name of America. Our forefathers who sacrificed their blood and sweat for the next generation in a way we have not had to sacrifice to date would blush at the downturn in America. Their basic goodness was evidenced by the great number of churches, hospitals, schools, and parks they left for their children's children. Their generation placed more emphasis on work than play.

President Clinton's promise to gays started an emotional time bomb ticking inside our armed forces. You will see the effects of its silent explosion soon in increased negative statistics unless there is a quick change. You might never hear noise from this atomic-like explosion but the damage will be equally terrible. Homosexual activists cannot be appeased, they truly know not what they ask. This bomb needs to be disarmed before it causes irreparable damage.

THE IMMORAL MINORITY

This small group of sodomites are a radical exception to the moral inclination of the majority. Though presently well positioned and entrenched to do major moral damage, they must be countered aggressively. Their numbers are much smaller than we are led to believe. But they do have a grasp of the military principles of mass and economy of force. Though less than two percent of our population they are well positioned politically, economically and geographically.

Our country can ill afford to grant them unrestricted recruiting rights — a fresh new recruiting ground inside our military gates. Consider their small numbers and the fact that their life spans statistically are thirty years shorter than ours. Sodomites unlike heterosexuals, can't become natural parents. They are not tied down in most cases to child rearing responsibilities. They pursue their adult pleasures and political agendas with far greater finances and fewer personal constraints. Sodomite leaders show misguided courage, driven more by their fear of death than by any conviction for the truth. Consider their morally outrageous actions during parades in obvious geographical strongholds such as New York, New Orleans, Seattle and San Francisco which are major tourist centers. A brilliant strategy! Their public demonstrations offend a sober majority who are too often bullied into silence. Peace is for most a more important value than truth.

Civilian politicians fear their frequent displays of wrath. But service members are trained for confrontation. We know that personal strength of character in the face of evil is paramount for success. Civilians by and large don't receive courage-building training to counter evil. The Marines have a tradition of speaking the truth as they see it inspite of popular opinion. Note that Lt. Colonel Pete Ellis's stand was not popular until after the attack on Pearl Harbor. There is a Marine saying that "When you see something new, ask an experienced Marine because he has been everywhere and seen everything." Will you help turn around our country's slide downward toward the lowest common denominator of moral values?

Civilian presidents should not be rewarding deviants for political support in election campaigns. Our military's core ethic should not be trifled with. Our military forefathers proved our country the greatest fighting force in world history with our Judeo-Christian core ethic. Certainly the direction we are now headed will unravel their magnificent efforts.

IS THE COLD WAR STILL HOT?

Fanatical forces that say they hate the achievement of Western civilization are at work inside and beyond our borders. Millions view us as "The Great Satan." This is a far more dangerous world environment than civilians realize. Down-sizing our military is based on the illusion that the Cold War is over. The Cold War is not over. It has just been decentralized. History shows that the weakening of a country's military force structure is never respected by potential adversaries.

I visited Afghanistan veterans in Russia in May of 1992 with the executive director of Point Man International, a support organization that assists veterans with post-military readjustment. It was a goodwill trip at their invitation to inform them about post-traumatic stress disorder (PTSD), and how to overcome this destroyer of men and their families.

During my visit I received an informal briefing from a knowledgeable Russian Afghanistan veteran who had a major concern with the decentralization of political power within the former Soviet Union. In eight of the eleven republics there is a Muslim majority. Many patriotic Russians were worried about what might happen if the military (nuclear) weapons in these Muslim regions fall into the hands of Muslim fanatics such as reside in Iran. In the view of many Russians, the world is a much more dangerous place than before the decentralization of Russian power.

These are dangerous times. The majority of Americans know nothing about the record of prior destroyed societies that took a similar moral route. Giving in to hedonistic (pleasure seeking) demands leads to experiencing the conquering sword once a nation becomes too weak-willed to resist.

I may be somewhat unique in my study of military history. I was a tactics instructor at the Basic Officer's School at Quantico, Virginia for three years. I later taught the history of warfare at a major land grant university for three years. On top of these formal teaching experiences, I grew up in the household of a war hero. Three other family members served in the Marine Corps obtaining the rank of colonel. Our collective combat experience covers WW I, the bandit wars in Central America, WW II, Korea, and Vietnam. My son, Steve, experienced limited combat in Haiti with the 2nd Battalion, 2nd Marines. I can say with authority the damage of such a policy change on individual military members and their families will make it difficult for our national survival.

From my research I conclude that most civilian experts in the fields of psychology, psychiatry, and sociology agree "privately" with my conclusions. Disintegration comes about when a society no longer is willing to keep its reprobates in check. President Clinton's trusted political advisers let him down on this issue. The general public may be too weighted down by personal concerns to effectively convey their heartfelt sickness over this "Welcome to the club invitation that results from lifting the ban against openly confessing homosexuals. The vast majority have an "inward knowing" about the right and wrong of this matter.

For years I've been taking notice of and have developed a respect for the writings and prophetic warnings of Reverend David Wilkerson of New York City. In one

183

of his newsletters he spoke of the self-destruction that America is in the midst of:

"For over a century and a half, America has not had a foreign troop on its soil. We haven't been invaded, attacked or bombed. We have sent our soldiers to fight in many wars, but always in other nations' land. Indeed, we have been spared...we have enjoyed peace and prosperity.

Even now, America breathes a sigh of relief because there no longer seems to be a nuclear threat. We believe communism is dead, that Russia will never again rise as a world power.

As of early 1996, Boris Yeltsin is still in power in Russia, but I believe he is a temporary leader. The Communist clique still exists and soon Yeltsin will be cast aside and a new, aggressive government will arise. The fact remains that 20,000 nuclear warheads are still at the former Soviets' disposal — most of them aimed at America! Recent pacts to reduce these warheads are not being honored as promised. We are reading more and more about hardliners in Russia. We can't act based on their stated intentions but must act based on their capabilities.

Right now China is like a giant, waking from its sleep. In just a few years Hong Kong will be turned over to China completely. It will become China's pearl city...a major money center and the gateway to wealth for Chinese markets. In time, China may bypass Japan as an economic power. Keep your eye on China!"

IS AMERICA SELF-DESTRUCTING?

I empathize with family members torn apart by a brother, sister, parent, or friend caught up in rebellion and sexual bondage. This is not a good reason however, to give in to their radical ideas and rebellious lifestyles.

It is a constant heartache for family members who love such a one. There is, however, one who can set such a prisoner free from the jailer. There is hope for those imprisoned by such perversions.

However, the military scene is no place for such people. In spite of the homosexual who hides his perversion and excels, then comes out of the closet; the military is too challenging an environment for those not strong physically, mentally, and morally. Homosexuals will only drag others down in time despite present contributions. Our national survival is at stake here.

The majority of homosexuals engaged in this behavior according to many studies use drugs and alcohol to lower their natural inhibitions. This is a clear indication of their true mental condition (bondage). Our military anti-drug policy is another reason for rejection of their demand for entrance.

From 1974 to 1976 I headed the Human Relations Leadership Training Section at Headquarters, Marine Corps. This training program was created as an adjunct to our traditional and informal leadership approach to lower the illegitimate barriers between service members created by distorted race, rank, age, sex, or ethnic-orientation outlooks. This was during a difficult time in the Corps' history. The training program largely achieved its purpose. During that era we had some members of the military service from various street gangs killing each other during their off-duty hours. Some were driven by hatred carried with them into the Corps from outside civilian neighborhoods. That same murderous spirit is still alive as human nature never changes. Big city police chiefs, as reported by Dr. Paul Cameron of the Family Research Institute, say that 50 percent of all murders are committed by the 1.7 percent of the population who are homosexual.

Those who think that a similar training program such as I supervised back in 1974 will work for this issue are unrealistic. Average men shouldn't be taught to respect something that is instinctively not respectable. Adopting an institutional lie does not change the truth. Remember the Nazi experiment in Germany. The truth is the truth. The bias of normal men towards homosexuality is natural. It may be for the wrong reason. A wrong reason can be changed to a better reason. But such prejudice is reasonable as it is life protecting. You cannot get good men to accept bad behavior that goes against their natural instincts under normal circumstances. Homosexuality, as we have seen is bad behavior. It is pure delusion to think that a massive reeducation program such as civilian leaders are attempting in the civilian world would be good for our military. It would not be good for the country it defends, or it would not even work and still preserve our nation. Such a program accommodates such a small number in this lifestyle. It is not worth the aggravation to the majority or the cost to implement.

There is an occasional military member who steps forward with an open confession he or she is gay. To those who control today's information centers and give these exhibitionists publicity this is news. The Gallup Poll clearly shows the majority of those in controlling positions within our society have views quite different from the silent majority.

Thank God, within this driven and lonely community many do want to honor God and in quiet desperation attempt to battle against these fleshly desires. In my view the battle is against an alien, demon spirit speaking thoughts to the one he torments. Few want to acknowledge that demons are real, and have the capacity to whisper such unholy thoughts because then they would have to get serious about God. The naive would rather claim such thoughts their own than entertain the thought that demons are real. Many homosexuals do have a right conscience concerning this sexual addiction and continue to struggle against this perversion by natural means not understanding that there is awesome supernatural help.

Why do sodomite leaders have a view so different from that of the majority? Why do many seek positions of political power? Most grew up in chaotic family environments. They naturally have a bias against traditional values because of a hypocritical adult/parent who preached one value while practicing an opposite one they hid from public view. Incest in a family of origin is horrible and very damaging. Victims grow up with a great need to be in control for the sake of others because of the out-of-control environment they experienced as children.

While I have great compassion for someone so victimized, the military is no place for them to work out self esteem. This arena is an attractive recruiting opportunity because of experimentation with alcohol and drugs by those away from home the first time. The potential for maleable sexual mates still in their formative years is unending because of personnel turnover. Traditional leaders are in the spiritual battle of their lives for the soul of America's military.

Those who join must continue to be encouraged through policy to lead a secret life. A loosening of this public policy will make it intolerable for those who are fighting to control unhealthy appetites. The bolder homosexuals will pressure the quieter ones to openly declare their preferences. They will have nothing to lose after becoming public. This will further break down the mores accountable for past successes. Western culture has succeeded more than any other culture in history precisely because of the Judeo-Christian ethic at its core.

The sexually bold, whether heterosexual or homosexual need to be discouraged. Alcohol use among many young service members in the formative years of their lives artificially lowers their inhibitions against trying something new. This makes them easy, obvious targets for implantation of this unholy spirit. This is a literal spirit we are dealing with. Lifting the ban will have the effect of turning many in a weak-willed moment (while drunk and off guard) into questioning whether they are homosexuals as the result of having sex forced on them. Shame from a rape experience creates identity crisis. We don't need such identity crises in the military.

Increasing liberalism and acceptance of such lifestyles will reduce our ability to recruit from the very families that produce those with the strongest moral characters. Parents who care for their sons and daughters won't want them exposed to such practices.

During the Vietnam conflict, key generals and admirals in political position to make a difference in President Lynden Johnson's fatal decision failed to influence him. Like Clinton, President Johnson had no military experience. President Johnson made the key decision to keep the reserves out of the war in Vietnam. That decision sent a powerful signal to our enemies that our country didn't have the will to win. It further hurt the morale of careerists like myself who faced multiple tours, and a much longer war lasting ten years. Most experts share my view that Johnson's presidential decision not to use reservists was the single most important reason victory was not achieved.

President Clinton appears not to have changed his attitude concerning this ban. A "rotting" process has begun. Like a tree that looks healthy on the outside, once the core is dead, the tree will quickly be dead all over.

Samson, in the Old Testament, was given supernatural strength from God. He told the wrong person, Delilah, in confidence thinking she was trustworthy. While he slept she cut his hair. He lost his supernatural strength. First the champion, then the nation came under the dominion of their mortal enemies.

We too can be quickly rendered defenseless to protect ourselves if we sleep through this vital national debate. We cannot afford to lose this verbal battle as the non-battle on the pros and cons of "no fault" divorce was lost. Like Samson we too will deserve the judgment that will befall us, as the result of sloth, a form of vileness. Take to heart the Bible's warning that, "The wicked strut about when what is vile is honored among men (Psalm 12:8)."

During the Vietnam War the most important battles were not fought in Vietnam, but on the TV screens and front pages of newspapers across America. The North Vietnamese hung on for dear life refusing to quit while our military defeated their best in battle after battle. Yet, critical civilians who didn't even realize their contributions were harmful lost the war of words in the U.S. thereby forfeiting our hard-fought actions in Vietnam. The verbal war of words back home proved to be the decisive factor.

THE DECIDING FACTOR

War is very confusing. Civilians were the deciding factor during Vietnam. Can soldiers be the deciding factor in this fight? Can we change the spirit of civilian compromise by standing up for what we believe? It must be done. Your contribution is vital. It will help ensure the margin necessary for victory in this crucial national civilian debate.

I am not advocating insurrection. Soldiers do have the right to express their political point of view in the appropriate non-military forum. I heard a navy lieutenant on Seattle's KVI-Radio's Mike Seagal show on January 19, 1996 promoting his gay point of view. We have the same right. Get involved in the debate.

This policy fight over the fitness of homosexuals to serve in our armed forces begun in earnest in 1993. The groundwork was carefully laid over many years. Our task will not be easy in changing the direction of the tide, but it must be done. We must recast what the majority believes on this matter. Your phone calls, letters and personal visits will make a difference. Legal actions must be your weapon of choice as you join in this great national debate. I feel it is equal in importance to the slavery debate prior to our American civil war. There is no solution short of total victory for one side. The truth can't be compromised. The two sides see this too differently. Compromise is not possible.

We can not afford for Act Up and Queer Nation to gain a foothold aboard military bases as did the Mau Mau and the KKK during the Vietnam era. We cannot afford for our military to be permanently polarized over such a matter. "A house divided cannot stand." Unity is the most important of the military's nine principles of war. For the sake of unity this emotional issue must be kept outside the military.

TELL THE TRUTH

The truth about the homosexual lifestyle is not being effectively told. Political leaders fear political and social retaliation from those who are dying of AIDS and have nothing more important to lose in that lifestyle. The liberal press has formed their opinion on this issue as they did during Vietnam. It differs from the majority of Americans. The key to positive change is for more of us to become vocal.

Rebels will flaunt their deviant morals at our nation. The nation that refuses to discipline rebels sinks into decay and oblivion alongside the rebels they should have disciplined. An unknown Marine author said, "When good men are no longer willing to fight, they will be overcome by evil from those who have nothing to lose."

Don't assume that there will be fairness from the media or the educational elite on this issue. For whatever reason they are largely deceived. They refuse to see the truth.

Yes, America seems to be self-destructing. Our problem is not Russia, China or the newly formed European United Nations. No, like Israel in the days of Hosea the prophet, America is disintegrating from within!

This is exactly what happened to the great British Empire. Just 350 years ago it was said, "The sun never sets on the British Empire." It was the most powerful, blessed and prosperous empire on the face of the earth.

But in 1659, Puritan watchmen were warning of the self-destruction of the British Empire. They were being raised up by God to warn of the self-destruction coming upon them because of rampant sin and godlessness! The British Empire was crumbling left and right, and what was ruining them was decay from within!

Thomas Hall wrote, "The sins of England I fear more than all the enemies of the world. It is not Spain, or Italy, France or Turkey, that I fear...it is the atheism, blasphemy, apostasy and the profaning of all that is holy, and contempt for the gospel... If anything destroys us, it is these abominations that reign among us."

When the empire crumbled, another Puritan writer, as quoted by Dave Wilkerson, commented, "God humbled us with sickness, plague, poverty and decay of our economy...we threw off the yoke of Christ and now we have on us the yoke of pestilence and disease."

History has proven again and again that the more powerful and prosperous a nation becomes, the more the people tend to turn away from God.

Our fathers who framed the Constitution agreed that all of America's blessings came "from God and His Christ." They warned that America would fall into corruption and shame if God was ever rejected. Oh, how far we have come from that today!

Think about what has happened in America: All the things we once gloried in have been turned into shame! We gloried in having the greatest economic power, best educational system, top industrial complex, strongest infrastructure, best medical system, greatest tolerance of other races. Yet now we have fallen behind in every category!

We gloried in our freedom and our religious heritage, and now those freedoms are being taken from us, one after another. Godless laws are being judicated by godless judges. Tax laws are being aimed at church properties. Special rights are being given to homosexuals.

Our once great health-care system is in ruin because of AIDS and other problems. Libraries and museums are closing because there are no funds to keep them open. Racial tension has hit its absolute peak.

The day is not far off when I will not be able to say what I am now saying without being sued or jailed. That is because homosexual power is already so strong in America, and it is taking great strides daily!

Gay rights are nothing new. The book of Judges says this was the cause of the burning of Gibeah, and the consequent death of 40,000 Israelites.

You remember Gibeah...the little Benjaminite town where a Levite came to bring home his runaway concubine. As the Levite slept in his host's home, a group of angry homosexuals took his concubine and sodomized her all night long. They were angry because they could

192

not have the Levite himself! The woman was dumped on the door stoop and died before morning.

What was the Benjaminites' response? They decided to defend the (homosexual) Gibeanites! These men from throughout the tribe of Benjamin, every warrior and strong man, husbands and businessmen—26,000 in all— gathered to defend the perverse "rights" of less than 700 homosexuals in Gibeah. Think of how jaded, abnormal and wicked these men must have been...forsaking wives, children, homes and land...to give their lives for a group of men who had gang-raped and killed a helpless woman!

God is not concerned about the small percentage of radical Act-Up homosexuals in America. Their number is infinitesimal. What God is more concerned about, and what is bringing God's judgment on America, is the growing number of homosexual defenders! They number in the millions!

God's wrath is upon us because the majority of Americans have forsaken their Christian values! God, believe it or not, is more concerned with what is living in our hearts than what is transpiring with the homosexuals and deviants that abound on this earth.

TAKE A STAND!

Patriot are you yet convinced that America is self-destructing? Are you motivated to stand up and speak out for the traditional values you believe in? Do you have courage of conviction? Our Founding Fathers intended for this republic to be ruled from intelligence not from weakness. Being silent during times of critical national debate does not help. My view is not as unpopular as you have been led to believe. The coward's path is silence during a time of critical debate. Be brave!

There is great need for men who will not cower to the special interests who think because they have power others must do as they say. All power is not legitimate power. Those who go along with the presently orchestrated political and educational flow deserve to be washed overboard. There won't be a turning around on this situation without pain. Real men aren't deterred from speaking the truth and acting on it because of the threat of pain. We can and must use the democratic process to recapture control of our country before it is too late.

In chapter eight of the book of Joshua once the sin was discovered and properly expelled from the camp, Joshua and his men overtook the city of Ai through an awesome ambush planned and executed under the direct leadership of God. We can win this battle if we adhere to Matthew 6:33, "But seek first His kingdom and His righteousness; and all these things shall be added to you." Be encouraged.

We are living in the age the prophet Joel foresaw. We will see some delivered out of unhealthy male bonding societies through the power of God. The sovereign power of God will be increasingly evident. Severe judgment, positive as well as negative, is coming. Don't miss out through compromise. Believe that God's promises are sure. Read books such as Malachi, Micah, and Hosea. Believe that you can do what Mark 16:17 says a believer can do. ("And these signs will accompany those who believe. In my name they will drive out demons; they will speak in new tongues...") You have every reason to be confident. God commands you to be confident. Don't embarrass your General (see Revelation 19) through cowardliness. Don't get caught up in unbelief based on what you see or hear. Get steeled in God's Word. Remain confident. Be courageous in the face of opposition.

There is deliverence from bondage, even if the awful bondage is the fear of speaking in public on an unpopular subject. The Lord is the Lord over all, even our problems. We must learn to trust in Him more and more.

As one last word on taking a stand. For military people who love and know Jesus as our personal Savior, it is important to know that God intends for us to conduct ourselves in specific ways. While making our views known, and speaking our minds about His truths, it is of utmost importance to remember that we are here only on a temporary enlistment. This battlefield called earth, is not our permanent duty assignment, and we must act accordingly. Someday we will all be "reassigned" in the afterlife, and what we have done here becomes meaningless.

God does not intend for us to only entangle ourselves in civilian life. "Suffer hardship with me, as a good soldier of Christ Jesus. No soldier in active service entangles himself in the affairs of everyday life, so that he may please the pursuits to the point of neglecting the call that he has on our lives (2 Timothy 2:3-4)." Stand up against sin, but beware that you don't get swept into "everyday affairs" of life, lest you get sidetracked, and eventually made ineffective in the spiritual war that permeates this mortal life.

God shows mercy to those in bondage if they are willing to cry out to Him with a repentant heart. Be ready, general judgment is coming. All who refuse to verbally restrain those who rebel against God's legitimate laws will be judged accordingly. Be sure the angels of God know clearly which side of the sin issue you are on. There is nothing better you can offer a person in bondage than "the hope of a high calling in Jesus Christ." A false love that refuses to correct or be corrected is the main pillar of this deception presently overcoming America on significant moral issues. All war is a form of rebellion. The key to avoiding the death angel during combat is to be found in the book of Revelations, chapter 12, verse 11: **"We overcome through the blood of the lamb and the word of our testimony unto death. "**

SEMPER FIDELIS!

"Before every man lies a wide and pleasant
road that seems right but ends in death."
Prov. 14:12 (LB)

Which path
will you
choose?

"Enter through the *narrow* gate.
For wide is the gate and broad is the road
that leads to destruction
and many enter through it.
But *small* is the gate and *narrow*
the road that *leads to life*
and only a *few* find it."
Matt. 7:13-14 (NIV)

Prophecy of George Washington

A 99-year old veteran of the winter of Valley Forge told this story for the last time in 1859 to Wesley Bradshaw, a writer, who published it that same year. "The last time I ever saw Anthony Sherman was on the fourth of July, 1859, in Independence Square. He was then ninety-nine years old, and becoming very feeble, but though so old, his dimming eyes rekindled as he gazed upon Independence Hall, which he came to visit once more.

'Let us go into the hall,' he said. 'I want to tell you of an incident of Washington's life — one which no one alive knows of except myself: and if you live, you will before long see it verified. Mark the prediction, you will see it verified.

From the opening of the revolution we experienced all phases of fortune, now good and now ill, one time victorious and another conquered. The darkest period we had, I think, was when Washington after several reverses, retreated to Valley Forge, where he resolved to pass the winter of 1877. Ah! I have often seen the tears coursing down our dear commander's care-worn cheeks, as he would be conversing with a confidential officer about the condition of his poor soldiers. You have doubtless heard the story of Washington's going to the thicket to pray. Well, it was not only true, but he used often to pray in secret for aid and comfort. And God brought us safely through the darkest days of tribulation.

One day, I remember it well, the chilly winds whistled through the leafless trees, though the sky was cloudless and the sun shone brightly. He remained in his quarters nearly all the afternoon, alone. When he came out I noticed that his face was a shade paler than usual, and there seemed to be something on his mind of more than ordinary importance. Returning just after dusk, he dispatched an orderly to the quarters of an officer, who was presently in attendance. After a preliminary conversation of about half an hour, Washington, gazing upon his companion with that strange look of dignity which he alone could command, said to the latter:

'I do not know whether it is owing to the anxiety of my mind, or what, but this afternoon, as I was sitting at this table engaged in preparing a dispatch, something in the apartment seemed to disturb me. Looking up, I beheld standing opposite me a singularly beautiful being. So astonished was I, for I had given strict orders not to be disturbed that it was some moments before I found language to inquire the cause of the visit. A second, a third, and even a fourth time did I repeat my question, but received no answer from my mysterious visitor except a slight raising of the eyes.

By this time I felt strange sensations spreading through me. I would have risen but the riveted gaze of the being before me rendered volition impossible. I assayed once more to speak, but my tongue had become useless, as if paralyzed. A new influence, mysterious, potent, irresistible, took possession of me. All I could do was to gaze steadily, vacantly at my unknown visitor.

Gradually the surrounding atmosphere seemed to fill with sensations, and grew luminous. Everything about me seemed to rarefy, the mysterious visitor also becoming more airy, and yet more distinct to my sight than before. I began to feel as one dying, or rather to experience the sensations which I have sometimes imagined accompany death. I did not think, I did not reason, I did not move.

All were alike impossible. I was only conscious of gazing fixedly, vacantly at my companion.

Presently I heard a voice saying, 'Son of the Republic, look and learn. 'While at the same time my visitor extended an arm Eastward.' I now beheld a heavy white vapor at some distance rising fold upon fold. This gradually dissipated, and I looked upon a strange scene. Before me lay, spread out in one vast plain, all the countries of the world — Europe, Asia, Africa, and America. I saw rolling and tossing between Europe and America the billows of the Atlantic. And between Asia and America lay the Pacific. 'Son of the Republic' said the same mysterious voice as before, 'look and learn.'

And this time the dark shadowy angel turned his face Southward. From Africa I saw an ill-omened specter approach our land. It flitted slowly and heavily over every town and city of the latter. The inhabitants presently set themselves in battle array against each other. As I continued looking I saw a bright angel on whose brow rested a crown of light, on which was traced the word 'Union.' He was bearing the American flag. He placed the flag between the divided nation and said. 'Remember, Ye are brethren.'

Instantly the inhabitants casting down their weapons, became friends once more and united around the national standard.

Again I heard the mysterious voice saying, 'Son of the Republic, Look and learn.' At this the dark shadowy angel placed a trumpet to his mouth, and blew three distinct blasts; and taking water from the ocean, he sprinkled it upon Europe, Asia and Africa.

Then my eyes beheld a fearful scene. From each of these continents arose thick black clouds that were soon joined into one. And throughout this mass there gleamed a dark red light by which I saw hordes of armed men. These men, moving with the cloud, marched by land and sailed by sea to America, which country was enveloped in the volume of cloud. And I dimly saw these vast armies devastate the whole country and burn the villages, towns and cities which I had seen springing up.

As my ears listened to the thundering of the cannon, clashing of swords, and the shouts and cries of millions in mortal combat, I again heard the mysterious voice saying, 'Son of the Republic, look and learn.' When the voice had ceased, the dark shadowy angel placed his trumpet once more to his mouth, and blew a long and fearful blast.

Instantly a light as of a thousand suns shone down from above me, and pierced and broke into fragments the dark cloud which enveloped America. At the same moment the angel upon whose head still shone the word union, and who bore our national flag in one hand and a sword in the other, descended from the heavens attended by legions of white spirits. These immediately joined the inhabitants of America, who I perceived were well-nigh overcome, but who immediately taking courage again, closed up their broken ranks and renewed the battle.

Again, amid the fearful noise of the conflict I heard the mysterious voice saying, 'Son of the Republic, look and learn.' As the voice ceased, the shadowy angel for the last time dipped water from the ocean and sprinkled it upon America. Instantly the dark cloud rolled back. Together with the armies it had brought, leaving the inhabitants of the land victorious.

Then once more, I beheld the villages, towns and cities springing up where I had seen them before, while the bright angel, planting the azure standard he had brought in the midst of them, cried with a loud voice: 'While the stars remain, and the heavens send down dew upon the earth, so long shall the Union last.' And taking from his brow the crown on which blazoned the word 'Union' he placed it upon the standard while the people kneeling down said, 'Amen.'

The scene instantly began to fade and dissolve, and I, at last saw nothing but the rising, curling vapor I at first beheld. This also disappeared, and I found myself once more gazing upon the mysterious visitor, who, in the same voice I had heard before, said. 'Son of the Republic, What you have seen is thus interpreted, three great perils will come upon the Republic. The most fearful for her is the third. But the whole world united shall not prevail against her. Let every child of the Republic learn to live for his God, his Land, and Union.' With these words the vision vanished, and I started from my seat and felt that I had seen a vision where in had been shown me the birth, the progress, and destiny of the United States.

'Such, my friends,' The venerable narrator concluded, 'were the words I heard from Washington's own lips, and America will do well to profit by them.'"

The Stars and Stripes
December 21, 1950
Reprint of article run in the U.S. War Veteran's paper, *The National Tribune*, in December 1880.

REFERENCES

Books:

Andrews, Robert. *The Family, Gods Weapon for Victory.* Mukilteo, Wash.: WinePress Publishing, 1995.

Burke, Davis. *Marine, The Life of Chesty Puller.* Boston.: Little, Brown & Co., 1962.

Griffith, Samuel B. *Sun Tzu, The Art of War.* New York.: Oxford University Press, 1963.

Dean, Chuck. *Nam Vet.* Portland, Ore.: Multnomah Press, 1990.

Duduman, Dumitru. *Through The Fire.* Fullerton, Calif.: Hand of Help, Inc., 1992.

Goulden, Joseph C. *Korea, The Untold Story.* New York.: Times Books, 1982.

Lejeune, Major General John A. *The Reminiscences of a Marine*. Philadelphia.: Dorrance & Co, 1930.

Lutzer, Erwin W. *Hitlers Cross*. Chicago.: Moody, 1995.

Marshall, S.L.A. *The Soldiers Load and the Mobility of a Nation*. New York.: William Morrow & Co, 1947.

MAGAZINES:

Ballendorf, Dirk Anthony. "Earl Hancock Ellis: The Man and His Mission." *Naval Institute Proceedings* (1983): 50.

Bradshaw, Wesley. "George Washington's Prophesy." *National Tribune* (1880), reprinted in *Stars & Stripes* (1950).

Davis, 1st Lt. Gordon M. "Dewey Canyon; All Weather Classic."*Marine Corps Gazette* (1969): 32.

Dodd, MSgt. J.D. USMC (Ret.). "The Vision of John A Lejeune." *Marine Corps Gazette* (1967): 36.

Gudel, Joseph P. "Homosexuality and Fiction." *Christian Research Journal* (1992).

Pierce, Lt. Col. P.N. USMC (Ret.). "The Unsolved Mystery of Pete Ellis." *Marine Corps Gazette* (1962): 34.